A Microcredit Alternative in South Asia

Microcredit took the development world by storm as a tool for poverty alleviation in the 1980s. After being hailed as a panacea, a few decades on it started being forcefully criticized based on its practice.

This book explores Akhuwat (literally brotherhood), a rapidly growing Pakistani NGO formed in 2001, which addresses the shortcomings of conventional microfinance. Its vision is of a society built on empathy and social solidarity, and its mission is that of creating self-sufficiency among the entrepreneurial poor. This book examines whether Akhuwat fulfils its promises of not pushing loans or encouraging clients to get on a debt treadmill and helping them to avoid high debt burdens by charging no interest and easing repayment terms. Conventional microcredit organizations are criticized for losing sight of the original mission of poverty alleviation by engaging in empire building, and Akhuwat's goal is to avoid this by embracing an alternative strategy of scaling up. Finally, this book also analyses Akhuwat's approach as being gender sensitive and embracing all religions, castes and ethnicities.

Based on fieldwork designed to assess if Akhuwat is the microcredit alternative it claims to be, this book will be of interest to scholars of poverty and development studies in general and microcredit in particular.

Shahrukh Rafi Khan is currently a Mount Holyoke College Research Associate. He has published extensively in refereed journals and authored and edited several books. His recent books include a *History of Development Economics Thought* (Routledge, 2014) and *Market as Means Not Master: Towards New Developmentalism* (Routledge, 2010).

Natasha Ansari is a Research Associate at the Collective for Social Science Research. She is one of the lead researchers on the Value Chains pillar for the research consortium Leveraging Agriculture for Nutrition in South Asia (LANSA) in Pakistan.

Routledge Studies in the Growth Economies of Asia

China's Economic Culture
The ritual order of state and markets
Carsten Herrmann-Pillath

Labour in the Clothing Industry in the Asia Pacific
Edited by Vicki Crinis and Adrian Vickers

The Chinese and Indian Corporate Economies
A comparative history of their search for economic renaissance and globalization
Rajeswary Ampalavanar Brown

The Diffusion of Western Economic Ideas in East Asia
Edited by Malcolm Warner

Employers' Associations in Asia
Employer collective action
Edited by John Benson, Ying Zhu and Howard Gospel

Business Leaders and Leadership in Asia
Ying Zhu, Shuang Ren, Ngan Collins and Malcolm Warner

Innovation, Investment and Intellectual Property in South Korea
Park to park
Ruth Taplin

A Microcredit Alternative in South Asia
Akhuwat's experiment
Shahrukh Rafi Khan and Natasha Ansari

For a full list of titles in this series, please visit www.routledge.com

A Microcredit Alternative in South Asia

Akhuwat's Experiment

**Shahrukh Rafi Khan
and Natasha Ansari**

LONDON AND NEW YORK

First published 2018
by Routledge
2 Park Square, Milton Park, Abingdon, Oxon OX14 4RN

and by Routledge
711 Third Avenue, New York, NY 10017

Routledge is an imprint of the Taylor & Francis Group, an informa business

© 2018 Shahrukh Rafi Khan and Natasha Ansari

The right of Shahrukh Rafi Khan and Natasha Ansari to be identified as authors of this work has been asserted by them in accordance with sections 77 and 78 of the Copyright, Designs and Patents Act 1988.

All rights reserved. No part of this book may be reprinted or reproduced or utilized in any form or by any electronic, mechanical, or other means, now known or hereafter invented, including photocopying and recording, or in any information storage or retrieval system, without permission in writing from the publishers.

Trademark notice: Product or corporate names may be trademarks or registered trademarks, and are used only for identification and explanation without intent to infringe.

British Library Cataloguing-in-Publication Data
A catalogue record for this book is available from the British Library

Library of Congress Cataloging-in-Publication Data
A catalog record for this book has been requested

ISBN: 978-0-8153-8685-8 (hbk)
ISBN: 978-1-351-17458-9 (ebk)

Typeset in Times New Roman
by Apex CoVantage, LLC

To the hundreds of brave and hard-working poor entrepreneurs we interviewed and the dedicated field staff we found serving them

Contents

Appendices viii
Preface ix

SECTION 1
Conceptual and institutional issues 1

1 Introduction 3
2 Altruism and faith-inspired giving 14
3 Altruism in Pakistan and Akhuwat's altruistic initiatives 25
4 Critiques of conventional microcredit 37
5 The Akhuwat interest-free microcredit model 57

SECTION 2
Empirical assessment 73

6 Akhuwat's microcredit alternative 75
7 Promoting self-sufficiency via enterprise 117
8 Policy issues 135

SECTION 3
Summary and conclusions 157

Index 163

Appendices

5.1	Expansion since inception	66
5.2	Akhuwat recovery rates since inception	67
5.3	Donated funds since inception	68
5.4	Percentage distribution of loan products	69
5.5	Akhuwat replications	70
6.1	Sample distribution by branch	95
6.2	Structured questionnaire	96
6.3	Focus group discussion questions	108
6.4	Focus groups by size and gender	109
6.5	Key informant interviews	110
6.6	Social appraisal forms	112
6.7	Business appraisal form	113
6.8	ROSCAs vs. Akhuwat's interest-free loans	114
7.1	Problems with designing an impact assessment study of Akhuwat's effectiveness	132
8.1	Proposed RCT (randomized control trial) on voluntary giving	150
8.2	Borrower suggestions for the organization	154

Preface[1]

In 1976 I chose the University of Michigan for graduate study because it still had a heterodox presence on the faculty, even though it was small and shrinking. Tom Weisskopf was the main draw for me, and I had hoped to work with him. A personal crisis during my studies there drew me back to my religious roots to seek stability. What appealed to me most about Islam, as I understood it, was the focus on personal freedom in religious practice and social justice for society.

Some aspects of Islam, in principle (according to many of its believers), support personal freedom and social justice, but the practice in many countries historically and currently is not consistent with these teachings. I was fortunate therefore that Tom Weisskopf agreed to chair my dissertation committee on Islamic Finance and Banking, and I could not have wished for a better, more open-minded, and rigorous scholar to learn from.[2]

I finished my dissertation in 1982 and returned to work in Pakistan. I was obligated by a bond to do this in exchange for the support I had received from the Ford Foundation and USAID mediated by the government of Pakistan.[3] I had intended to continue to work on Islamic economics notwithstanding the bemusement, tolerance or hostility of various friends. However, the timing was not right.

Pakistan was being run by a military dictator (General Zia-ul-Haq, 1979–1988), who may have been devout in his own way, but who also used Islamic symbols and policy for his regime's political legitimacy. Islamic scholarship was at this time associated with the patronage of this military dictator, and careerism in the field was rife and unpalatable. The last straw for me was when a paper I had written for a conference could not be accepted without being vetted by the Council of Islamic Ideology. So I turned to other topics instead.

It was about three decades later that a thoughtful student and my co-author, Natasha Ansari, also from Pakistan, asked me to supervise her senior thesis at Mount Holyoke College. This book has emerged from her time at Akhuwat, Lahore, in the summer of 2012. Using altruism to conceptually frame Akhuwat's Islamic microcredit alternative and drawing on her fieldwork, she wrote a highly successful senior thesis. Notwithstanding her concerns about how successfully the organization would in fact scale up, she persuaded me that further research based on systematic fieldwork was warranted.

We have drawn here on the Akhuwat website to briefly introduce it to the reader. We have devoted Chapter 5 to a detailed review of the organization, its mission, its functioning and the changing nature and scale of its operations.[4] The idea of Akhuwat emerged among a group of friends at the Lahore Gymkhana Club in 2001.[5] During this conversation, the exorbitant interest rates charged by microfinance programs claiming to alleviate poverty were being criticized. The idea of initiating an interest-free microfinance program was brought forth as a challenge; at that point, no one present foresaw the shape this experiment would eventually take. One of the friends pledged a donation of Rs. 10,000 to initiate the project, while another friend, Dr. Amjad Saqib, utilized that donation to make an interest-free loan.[6]

The first loan of Rs. 10,000 was given to a widow who was striving to earn a decent living via self-employment. She was neither begging nor soliciting charity but merely needed a helping hand. By utilizing and returning that loan within a period of six months as agreed, she reinforced the belief among the group of friends in the integrity of the poor when they are helped in a trusting and respectful way. The success of the first loan brought in more donations, and the group of friends became convinced of the viability of a possible venture into interest-free microfinance – hence, Akhuwat was born, with this group of friends forming the first Board of Governors and Dr. Amjad Saqib serving as the first Executive Director.

Akhuwat derives its name from the Arabic word *mwakhaat*, or 'brotherhood.' In Islamic tradition, the earliest example of this was exhibited in the fraternity formed by the *Ansars* (citizens of Medina) and the *Muhajireen* (or migrants from Mecca) who had escaped to Medina to avoid religious persecution.[7] Inspired by the spirit of compassion and generosity that induced the Medinites to share half of their wealth with the migrants, Akhuwat seeks to invoke this concept of brotherhood through its operations.

For Akhuwat, the metaphor of brotherhood entails the creation of a system based on mutual support in society. Further, the mechanism for attaining this objective, Akhuwat's mission, is giving and the belief is that this is part of the process of attaining *bhaichara*. While *bhaichara* literally translates into brotherhood, the essence is social solidarity based on other consciousness or empathy.[8] Microfinance is only one of the tools, albeit a powerful one, employed by Akhuwat to attain its objective of social solidarity and empathy. In Islamic tradition, the principle that emerged from *mwakhaat* was giving a hand-up to enable individuals to become self-sufficient by manufacturing and trading; thus, microcredit fits in well with Islamic economic philosophy.

One of Akhuwat's primary deviations from conventional microfinance is that it charges no interest rates to be consistent with the Islamic ban on *riba* (narrowly interpreted to mean interest – see Chapter 8 for a fuller account). Akhuwat has also drawn on the Islamic tradition of *Qarz-e-Hassn*, which entails helping someone in need with interest-free loans, a practice viewed as preferable to charity and doles as indicated above. While drawing on the tradition of *Qarz-e-Hassn*, Akhuwat has over time incorporated many of the best practices and lessons learnt from conventional microfinance from across the globe as well.

In its initial years, Akhuwat was simply engaged in a philanthropic exercise to see how interest-free microfinance would fare. Over time, however, donations greatly increased, and with this momentum the movement accelerated far beyond the expectations of its founders. By 2003, donations to Akhuwat had reached Rs. 1.5 million with the loan-recovery rate sustained since inception at 100 percent. Consequently, it was decided to formalize the organization, and 'Akhuwat' was registered under the Societies Registration Act of 1860. The first branch was opened at Township, Lahore, and operations began to expand.

With the passage of time, Akhuwat's branches were opened throughout the country, loan products were diversified, the clientele was expanded, and the message of Akhuwat began to spread rapidly. The movement was supported by individual philanthropic donations and volunteerism, and in the initial years no foreign donations were solicited so as not to dilute the sense of borrower/member[9] ownership. However, since Akhuwat was rapidly growing, it became necessary to revise and refine the operational methodology of the organization. In this regard it has been very flexible and has constantly adapted while not compromising its core mission.

In the absence of interest rates and due to the charging of a minimal registration fee from borrowers (in 2011, the registration fee was Rs. 100 / US$1.14), every effort was made to ensure that operation costs were kept very low. Extreme simplicity in operational activities, plain offices, use of religious places for meetings, and high levels of volunteerism in the workforce ensured that Akhuwat realized this goal. Its operational practices followed four core principles, which in time became the defining features of the Akhuwat model: interest-free loans, use of religious places, volunteerism and transforming borrowers into donors.

As the demand for Akhuwat's products grew, Akhuwat adopted a dual-track approach to expansion. On the one hand, Akhuwat continues to expand its operation in a traditional manner by opening up new branches in different cities and towns across Pakistan based on community solicitations leading to follow-up investigations by Akhuwat staff to ascertain the suitability of opening a branch in that location. On the other hand, it invites other organizations to replicate the Akhuwat model, with Akhuwat training the staff and assisting in the initial set-up. These replications are urged to strive to become local successes as opposed to emerging as branded clones of Akhuwat. Thus, unlike some development NGOs, Akhuwat has sought to avoid the empire-building trap where scale gets tied to resources and vice versa with the core mission clouded by organizational compulsions.

Based on the four core principles identified above, the operational methodologies continue to be refined and documented. International microfinance institutions and philanthropists also began to show interest in introducing Akhuwat in their own countries, and national and international academic institutions started incorporating its practices into their curricula. The founders envisage that the message of Akhuwat will spread beyond Pakistan and South Asia in the coming years. From its modest beginnings as a philanthropic experiment, Akhuwat has now emerged as a movement that continues to make a significant difference in the many lives it touches. As researchers, we too were touched by the organization and were moved to investigate its operations and claims. While we were broadly sympathetic to Akhuwat's mission, we have attempted as social scientists to minimize bias and to ask the hard questions and document honestly the findings.

Special thanks are due to Fatima Rasheed, Aleem Emmanual, Abu Bakr Siddiqui, Shakeel Ishaq, Shahzad Akram and Hassan Qadeer of Akhuwat for facilitating our research requests. Thanks are also due to Saqib Jaffery for taking an active interest in this project and offering thoughtful feedback and to Kazim Raza Awan for raising excellent questions. We are indebted to Mehlab Jameel for sharing her perspective with us regarding Akhuwat's work with the transgender community and providing valuable feedback on Chapter 3 in this regard. We are grateful to Haris Gazdar and the Collective for Social Science Research for generously allowing fieldwork time and the use of office facilities to Natasha Ansari. We are grateful to Zainab Khalid for hosting her during the pre-testing of this work in Islamabad. We are grateful to Rebecca Onyango and Mehreen Ali for valuable research assistance.

We are extremely grateful to the anonymous reviewer for extensive, critical but always valuable comments. We think that the time and care devoted to the review greatly improved the manuscript, and the generosity shown by the reader is in the best academic tradition. While it was up to us to make the most of the guidance provided, we were moved by this generosity, which is very much in the giving spirit of the organization we were studying. We are also grateful to the second reviewer, who carefully evaluated if we had addressed the first reviewer's comments adequately and in addition provided helpful suggestions.

Finally, we are grateful to Dorothea Schaefter of Routledge for her belief in this project and the patience she exhibited in carrying forward the review process. We would also like to acknowledge Lily Brown of Routledge for efficiently seeing the project through its subsequent stages. Thanks to Suzanne Sherman Aboulfadl for excellent indices for this and earlier books.

Notes

1 This preface starts in the first person, even though this is a co-authored book, to explain its genesis. The initiation of the co-authorship with Natasha Ansari is subsequently explained.
2 Many years later I had the opportunity to thank Tom Weisskopf by suggesting a Festschrift in his honor to Robert Pollin. This idea received a warm reception, and Robert Pollin and Jennette Wicks-Lim (also Tom's student) executed the project brilliantly, and this led to a book edited by them on aspects of Professor Weisskopf's work, including an essay by him in 2013.
3 Even as a critic of many US foreign policy positions over the years, I have remained grateful and indebted for the generosity of US taxpayers and this policy of enlightened self-interest.
4 www.akhuwat.org.pk/
5 Lahore is the capital of Punjab Province, the most populated and prosperous of Pakistan's four provinces.
6 The Pakistani Rupee to USD exchange rate in 2001 was about 55.5.
7 We suggested in a personal interview with Dr. Amjad Saqib, and also further on in this book (Chapter 8), that brotherhood in a literal sense excludes almost half of humanity and that the essence of Akhuwat is social solidarity and empathy and that this aspect of the organization's mission statement should be emphasized. The idea of *behenchara* (sisterhood) emerged from this discussion and was subsequently popularized in Pakistan in 2016, on social media particularly, via the "Girls at *Dhabas* (roadside food stalls)" initiative, of which Natasha Ansari is a co-founder. This initiative seeks to reclaim public space for women and progressive organizations like Akhuwat could help this agenda by being sensitive to terminology.
8 While Akhuwat's focus is on humans, logically this empathy extends to all species.
9 The organization prefers the term 'members' instead of 'borrowers' or 'beneficiaries' to infuse a sense of participation and to downplay hierarchy.

Reference

Pollin, R. and J. Wicks-Lim, eds. 2013. *Capitalism on Trial: Explorations in the Tradition of Thomas E. Weisskopf* (Northampton: Edward Elgar).

Section 1
Conceptual and institutional issues

1 Introduction

Akhuwat can contribute to a much needed debate in Pakistani society; one that is currently repressed.[1] While election research demonstrates that the public in Pakistan is not enamored with a forceful imposition of religiosity, nonetheless polls show most view themselves as religious and identify with Islam. In 2006, Gallup Pakistan asked: "Should religion be separate from politics?" Fifty-three percent replied in the affirmative, 18 percent were not sure and only 29 percent thought that religion should not be separate from politics.

These views were even more strongly reflected in questions about religious decrees that affect personal life. In response to the question "Some people think that the *hijab* (head covering) by Muslim women should be made compulsory while others are of the view that it is a matter of personal choice and willingness. Should the *hijab* be enforced?" In response, 83 percent thought it is a matter of personal choice, 10 percent said that they did not know and only 7 percent stated that the *hijab* should be enforced.[2]

On the issue of religiosity, Gallup Pakistan found in a survey of youth (18–30) that living according to religious doctrines was very important for 66 percent and only 3 percent considered it to be not important at all.[3] Thus while religiosity is high among the population, the majority view faith and religion to be a personal issue.

However, religiosity among the public creates a ratchet effect in social legislation, such as alcohol prohibition or blasphemy laws (also see below), which deepen and entrench social fissures because such concessions to an extremist vision of Islam are difficult to reverse. Both popularly elected politicians and military dictators alike have used religions symbols and policy for legitimacy. Once a concession to intolerance is made, reversing that becomes seemingly impossible in the face of popular religiosity and orthodoxy buttressed by militancy.

Orthodoxy or fundamentalism is a reference to those who subscribe to traditionalist interpretations of Islamic law. Modernists or progressive interpretations include those believing in the separation of religion and state.[4] The suppression of liberty, such as via state imposition of intolerant social legislation, breeds resentment among liberals (both religious and secular) while the orthodox view as paltry the state's concessions to them.[5]

The orthodox view the doors to debate as shut and view the Islamic tradition of *ijtihad* (independent reasoning to arrive at truth in religious matters)[6] as heresy, while secular liberals find such a debate irrelevant and view the orthodox with disdain. However, in our view it is necessary for the modernists to engage since having popular veneration, street power and militant backing make the orthodox far from irrelevant.

Unfortunately the ability of orthodoxy to harness street power and militant violence creates a climate of oppression not conducive to debate and discussion. The case of a prominent modernist Islamic Scholar, Fazl ur Rahman Malik, comes to mind. He was invited back from teaching in the West by Pakistan's first military dictator, General Mohammed Ayub Khan (1958–1969), to head the Central Institute of Islamic Research. Traditionalists engaged in ad hominem attacks rather than address the scholarly logic of his positions, and he resigned his post.[7] This was Pakistan's loss, and Fazl ur Rahman went on to establish the Center of Middle Eastern Studies as a full professor at the University of Chicago.

Pakistan's third dictator, General Zia-ul-Haq (1978–1988), decided unilaterally to Islamize the country and imposed a highly orthodox version of Islam on the population. Government employees and the wider population became subject to social pressure to pray in the work places, women were expected to cover their heads and don shawls or conservative clothing, eating publicly was prohibited during *Ramzan* (month of fasting), and overt practice and expressions of religiosity were encouraged and rewarded such as in securing promotions. The dictator announced that senior promotions would be awarded to those who conformed. Western culture was discouraged on state-run TV, and movie going was subjected to increased taxes. For many, religion went from being a matter of personal faith to a public show of piety responding to state and social pressure.

School curricula were Islamized, and *madrassa* (religious schools) education, on a separate track, was encouraged; and it is the proliferation of these schools with Middle Eastern funds that are viewed as becoming the hotbed of the Afghan and Pakistani Taliban. Social legislation included the *Hadood* Ordinance for adultery, fornication and crimes (including stoning, whipping and amputations). The initiatives for Islamizing the economy included compulsory *zakat* (wealth) tax, though modernist Islamic scholars argue that giving is intended to be voluntary as a form of striving to attain spiritual purity. Interest-free banking (most agreed this is an eyewash) was introduced to conform to the ban on usury or *riba* (see Chapter 8).[8]

It was not possible for democratic regimes that followed to reverse any of these Islamic initiatives. In fact Zia-ul-Haq's protégé, Nawaz Sharif, unsuccessfully attempted to declare himself Amir-ul-Momineen (leader of the faithful) and introduce sweeping constitutional amendments to entrench Islamization in his second elected bout in office (1997–1999). During his most recent tenure (2013–2017), Sharif did not attempt such radical restructuring, though this alliance with religious parties remained strong. The public mood shifted away from support of extreme Islamic ideology after the Taliban groups subjected the local population to incessant and brutal acts of terror.

So Pakistan has not engaged in a much needed debate, and little renaissance in Islamic thinking is evident. This is despite the Qur'an's (the main source of Law in Islam) emphasis that enforcing a particular perspective is not called for. There are numerous verses in the Qur'an indicating the Prophet's role to be only that of a warner[9] (7:184, 7:187, 11:2, 11:12, 13:7, 15:89, 16:82, 17:105, 22:49, 27:92, 28:46, 29:50, 33:45, 34:28, 34:46, 35:23, 36:6, 38:65, 42:48, 46:9, 48:8, 50:51, 64:12, 67:26), guide (16:64, 43:52), emissary (17:93), reminder (16:44), witness (22:78), messenger (13:40, 29:18, 36:3), conveyor (29:55), herald of glad tidings (18:56, 33:45, 34:28, 35:24, 36:11), bringer of truth (23:70, 33:45), beacon of light (33:45) but not that of a guardian (17:55), or keeper (10:108, 42:48), or responsible for others' conduct (42:6). Nor was he sent with the "power to determine (human) fate (17:55)." As indicated in the Qur'an, apart from this role as a messenger "he is but a mortal" like other humans (17:94, 18:110, 41:6), "not a prodigy" and unaware of "what will be done with him" (46:9), and reckoning or requiting belongs only to God (13:40, 45:14).

Another related recurring theme is that of avoiding the use of force in matters of faith. The Prophet was informed that "your mission is only to give warning: It is for Us to do the reckoning" (10:98) and that God "needs none to defend Him from humiliation" (17:105). Another verse in the same vein is: "He that fights for God's cause fights for himself. God needs no man's help" (29:6).[10] More explicitly, believers are informed that there should be "no compulsion in religion" (2: 256) or that humans should be called "to the path of your Lord with wisdom and kindly exhortation" (16:126). Thus, once humans are confronted with the truth from the Lord, humanity is told: "Let him who will, believe in it, and him who will, deny it" (18:28).

Citing chapter and verse is tricky business as Shakespeare informed us so long ago in *The Merchant of Venice*. His celebrated quote, spoken by Antonio, is: "The devil can cite Scripture for his purpose." Yet, the purpose here is simply to challenge a trenchantly held position by militant orthodoxy that it has the monopoly on religious truth and the right to dictate and indeed "force this down people's throat" as the Pakistani military dictator, Zia-ul-Haq, stated he was justified in doing.

6 *Conceptual and institutional issues*

The extremists bury prescriptions privileging choice and instead practice oppression. This is what makes Akhuwat important, particularly since it taps into enlightened Islamic traditions with practice (rather than just words) and good work, as prescribed by Islam (and also other religions), is much more difficult to stamp out. But with the emphasis on "good work," Akhuwat brings to the table an inclusive and enlightened interpretation of what it means to be a Muslim and one that is consistent with the verses cited above. For Akhuwat, being a Muslim means accepting all faiths and a religious practice that emphasizes altruism, volunteerism and giving. Accordingly, Chapter 2 of this book explores altruism in the broader economics literature to contextualize the Islamic perspective on it and to arrive at a working definition that we can use to evaluate Akhuwat's policy in this regard.

Lindblom (1977) classified the mix of mechanisms governing political economic systems into authority, markets and "preceptoral (using norms to guide social behaviour)." The complexion of the system is identified by the predominant mechanism such as market for the capitalist liberal democracies and centralized planning for socialist states. Based on this classification, Akhuwat predominantly relies on the preceptoral mechanism which involves "'educating' the population towards the right socio-economic conduct" by example (Khan, 1987, p. 16).

Akhuwat attempts to make altruism and volunteerism operational at various levels in all its initiatives or interventions including microcredit. Other than microcredit, Akhuwat has also diversified into various other activities mentioned briefly below and described in more detail in Chapter 3. It encourages successful borrowers to offer 'internships' to new borrowers. Akhuwat volunteers also run social delivery programs like setting up libraries at orphanages and organize field trips for students from low-income schools and orphanages. It also has training, education and health initiatives.

Akhuwat Institute of Social Enterprise & Management is a state-of-the-art research and training center and also contains an incubation center for microenterprises. Potential entrepreneurs (artificial jewelry making, embroidery, spare parts manufacturing, electrical items, clothes stitching, leather products) undergo capacity building including in marketing, financial services, advertising, product design and improvement and forward/backward integration. The plan is to provide training and angel investment for promising projects. The pilot project is to be gradually scaled up to eventually cater to 500 micro-enterprises. The hope here is that these enterprises will create livelihoods, and they are expected therefore to operate at a larger scale than the self-employment it facilitates via its microcredit initiative.

By mid-2016, more than 27,000 students had benefited from Akhuwat's various education initiatives. It also supported students from income-poor backgrounds who gained admission to Pakistan's top educational institutions. It has plans to found an Akhuwat University for bright students from income-poor backgrounds. Akhuwat's Internship and Leadership program has been training 60 interns per year through a rigorous and practical four-week module which acquaints the interns to multiple organizations in the development sector.

Akhuwat Clothes Bank collects clothes donated by more-prosperous families; and after repair, cleaning, and packaging, these are distributed as gifts to needy individuals. In partnership with a non-profit organization, Fountain House, it has also established a program for the social reintegration of the *khwaja sira* (transgender) community members who run this program. The program has several intended stages, starting with social engagement and provision of a small income supplement (Rs.1,150) to the most vulnerable. In its final form, Akhuwat and Fountain House hope to be able to reintegrate the *khwaja siras* they work with into society as equal citizens.

Conceptually, Akhuwat seeks to build community based on individual responsibility. This differs from other grassroots initiatives based on collective action. We think both initiatives are welcome and are not mutually exclusive. Successful collective action is often premised on the role played by a local social activist, often in partnership with a development NGO, who volunteers time and energy to help mobilize the community for projects that enhance community well-being. The difference is one of emphasis and practice. Akhuwat's social philosophy is that all individuals should offer more as a solution to social problems than their contribution to problems and so the spirit of the social activist should be embodied in all as an ideal.

Akhuwat is also significant for us because it claims to address the many criticisms of microcredit.[11] The latter is still widely viewed as an important development initiative for poverty alleviation. Critics have charged that both the microcredit organizations and the instruments used are questionable. The contention is that even non-profit microcredit organizations pursue their own agenda at the expense of women. Peer group pressure designed to tap into and build social capital actually destroys it. Social capital is cynically used as a mechanism to reduce transaction costs in recovering loans but in the process sets community members against each other since loans become inter-dependent within peer groups formed to facilitate loan recovery. If the loan to the next person in the peer group is dependent on the repayment of a loan by another member, it creates the incentive for intrusive monitoring within peer groups, even of each other's consumption patterns. Thus, social capital is systematically undermined given the way incentives are structured. It also creates household discord whereby male members, often the ones using the loans, pressure females to secure more loans even if they themselves are responsible for non-payment of the earlier loans. Finally, it does little to promote genuine entrepreneurship.

A large part of the feminist critique of microcredit is that instead of empowering women, it intensifies their oppression whether or not they use the loans themselves. Field officers capitalize on the lack of female mobility and their "docility," compared to males, to pressure them for repayments. If they pass on the loans to male household members, they are still responsible for repayments and are subject to organizational pressure. If they use the loans themselves, they now have another activity in addition to all the household work since males refuse to do "women's work."

It is further alleged that founders and senior management of the organizations are more concerned with empire building based on donor funding, and organizational growth, including staff size, is viewed as a marker of success. Scaling up gets donor attention and more funds but reduces due diligence and hence results in more troubled borrowing. The initial objective of poverty alleviation becomes subordinated to organizational growth impulses and by the organizational concern with recovery rates, even if this means using harsh loan recovery methods.

In addition to organizational growth, financial sustainability is another marker of success, again divorced from the original objective of poverty alleviation. Since peer groups are self-selected and since there is a high premium on avoiding default, the poorest, viewed as poor loan risks, are excluded. Even non-profit microcredit organizations charge a high interest rate arguing that they need to recover high transaction costs. They also encourage clients to continue to borrow, often inducing them to get onto a debt treadmill. When multiple organizations serve the same area, individuals borrow from one to pay loans secured earlier from another organization.

In the Pakistani context, Najma Sadeque, a prominent feminist, human rights advocate and op-ed columnist wrote a scathing critique of the important Pakistani microfinance institutions in the country for a major English language daily (*The Nation*, December 25, 2013). The only organization that escaped this critique and instead came in for praise was Akhuwat. We were intrigued by this praise from a noted progressive and feminist and thought that more rigorous research was needed to evaluate this praise.

Microcredit is a key element of the government's poverty alleviation strategy with the Pakistan Poverty Alleviation Fund (PPAF) the lead publically supported apex civil society organization. The PPAF claims to have made eight million microcredit loans since its inception in 2000 through November 2016.[12] Given this emphasis on microcredit, the evaluation of an Islamic alternative is important since one of us confronted great hostility to the giving and taking of interest among the population while doing fieldwork for another project.[13]

The current central and provincial administration in the Punjab (2013–) is certainly supporting Akhuwat's initiative. The Chief Minister of the Punjab visited the opening of an Akhuwat branch to give the organization his blessing and the last Prime Minister initiated a Rs. 3.5 billion Interest Free Loan Scheme to support micro enterprises as a small part of the PPAF, hence also endorsing the Akhuwat model. Even though Akhuwat now has national prominence, to date there has been only one evaluation by an academic consultant in a comparative context.[14]

As stated earlier, Akhuwat claims that it has managed to address many of the criticisms summarized above and reviewed in detail in Chapter 4. We earlier indicated that Chapter 2 is devoted to a discussion of altruism to contextualize Akhuwat's microcredit and other interventions. In Chapter 3 its non-microcredit altruistic interventions are briefly reviewed in the broader context of altruism in Pakistan. The rest of the book (Chapters 5–8) is devoted to Akhuwat's microcredit intervention.

In Chapter 5 we frame Akhuwat's microcredit model as an alternative. We start with an overview of the organization's mission and vision, turn next to the organizational structure and how it operates and then turn to Akhuwat's interest-free microcredit model. In Chapters 6 and 7 we explore, based on our fieldwork, if Akhuwat's claims are well founded and if it is managing to realize its mission statement and its vision.

In Chapter 6, after explaining our research design and sampling, we explore whether Akhuwat could be viewed as a success based on several indicated criteria including the perceptions of borrowers. Our findings suggest that this is overwhelmingly so, and we speculate on the causes of this success. Further, we explore if Akhuwat is managing to attain its vision and finally whether it has successfully addressed the shortcomings of conventional microcredit as it claims to have done.

One of the governing assumptions of microcredit is that all individuals have the ability to be entrepreneurs, and indeed conceptually this is what the success of microcredit was premised on.[15] Akhuwat implicitly assumes some distribution of entrepreneurship in the population but not that each individual is capable of entrepreneurship as does the Grameen model. Thus, it very carefully vets applications to back ventures with the potential of becoming growth drivers in urban shanty towns and rural areas. Akhuwat's stated mission is to "alleviate poverty by empowering socially and economically marginalized families through interest free microfinance and by harnessing entrepreneurial potential, capacity building and social guidance." We explore in Chapter 7 how successful the organization has been in attaining its mission statement based on field observations, survey responses, group discussions, key informant field interviews and case studies.

Chapter 8 is devoted to a discussion of microcredit policy issues that emerged from our empirical research. While much of what is contained in this chapter is directed at Akhuwat, the issues have broader relevance for

10 Conceptual and institutional issues

microcredit organizations. Some of these policy issues include how Akhuwat interacts with and transforms local culture. There are potential conflicts between organizational and social needs including on issues of loan size, group loans and group dynamics, and selectivity vs. inclusivity. We consider operational issues including reconciling hierarchy with *bhaichara*, use of religious spaces, nature of monitoring and the motivation of field staff. We reflect on the nature of pragmatism evident in Akhuwat's policy formation. More sensitive policy issues pertain to the adoption of the name Akhuwat, the partners the organization works with, its interpretation of *riba* (as interest) and its solicitation of donations. We explore its accounts to discuss sustainability issues and finally summarize key suggestions from the field.

The lead author has attempted to evaluate prominent development NGOs in Pakistan, and twice these attempts were aborted, once literally on the night before the fieldwork was to begin. The sticking point was our insistence on independent evaluation with free, open and unaccompanied access based on representative sampling. The top management of one of Pakistan's leading development NGOs insisted that they be given authorship of the study, which would have compromised the actual or perceived validity of the research. Akhuwat was refreshing in this regard. They welcomed a rigorous evaluation, were extremely forthcoming throughout and imposed no conditions that might compromise the integrity of the research.

We fielded several proposals for our modest fieldwork expenses (about US$5,000) without success. One issue could simply be hostility in the West to the subject of an Islamic initiative. Another issue could be our inability to persuade potential donors of the value of this study, and one claimed it was too academic. One donor (the International Growth Center, Pakistan Office) was encouraging but wanted us to frame the study as an RCT (randomized control trial). These have become the rage in empirical research for impact assessment following the funding and proselytizing on this method by the J-Pal at the MIT.[16]

We refused to comply with this request because we viewed it as a form of methodological fundamentalism but more so because, for reasons mentioned in Appendix 7.1, we were not persuaded it would be a useful exercise. As it turns out, we have recommended an RCT exercise in our policy chapter (Appendix 8.1) on the issue of making altruism operational, but this we view as having emerged organically from our research.

In fact our concern with RCTs is that they do not seem to emerge from any conceptual framework. In addition they are often sterile, as much of the econometric research in economics often is, with its fixation on increasingly more sophisticated ways of estimating parameters of questionable value. In our view, valuable social knowledge requires painstaking fieldwork that can result in a systemic and institutional understanding of the subject.

Also, given the variation across sites we confronted in the field, we view RCTs as virtually impossible to replicate or generalize from. However, our main concern is that they seem to be narrow and technocratic, too costly, ignore systemic problems, and thus perhaps inadvertently rid economics research of a broad social science perspective. Without a conceptual framework and institutional detail, one may be left at best with an efficiently conducted but barren impact assessment and at worse junk social science masquerading as the equivalent of natural science.

In private communication, Saqib Jafarey (currently Professor of Economics, City University, London) eloquently pointed to another problem associated with RCTs: "what seems to have happened with RCTs is that they have stood even quantitative research on its head: it is now increasingly difficult, or even impossible, to publish research that starts with an avowedly important question and then makes the most of whatever data and other tools can be brought to bear on it. Now, it is the data collection technique that comes first and only those questions that can be studied via an RCT are considered legitimate for study." This research purports to engage in more traditional empirical social research starting with a conceptual framework, research questions emanating from them, and then an investigation of those questions.

We view Akhuwat as part of "a giving economy."[17] A giving economy is much broader than the activities that civil society organizations like Akhuwat are engaged in. However, Akhuwat certainly demonstrates one form of the implementation of a giving economy. In our view, voluntarism and giving does not obviate the need for a tax-based state supported social safety net, but it may reduce the extent of the need for one. Further, we think that it can be a critical element in less-prosperous societies which have limited resources and weak tax administrations. Ultimately we see this aspect of a giving economy as complementing rather than substituting for collective action. We use collective action here in the broadest interpretation of the term, i.e. paying taxes for the collective need with redistribution being a socially endorsed part of the social contract.

Higher tax collections that are needed to deliver social welfare are a chicken-egg dilemma. The state can establish fiscal credibility by delivering services and demonstrating good use of funds to improve the fiscal effort. But delivering services requires funds. Until this conundrum is resolved and prosperity attained, other forms of giving or sharing can play a more prominent role.

Notes

1 A good example of an attempt at engagement nonetheless was the film *Khuda Ka Liye* (which literally translates into 'For God's Sake'), written, directed and

produced by Shoaib Mansoor. A key lyric in a song protests, "He is our God too," as a direct challenge to fundamentalists who have assumed a self-righteous monopoly of being the guardians of the true Islam. The validity of this position in Islamic Law is addressed later in the introduction.
2 www.gallup.com.pk/Religion.php.
3 http://gallup.com.pk/News/ReportFinalDraftVotersStudy2012.pdf, p. 5, p. 24.
4 Refer to Khan (1987, chapter 1) for a fuller discussion.
5 The overlay of class and religiosity further enhance social tensions.
6 This refers to the right to debate on social and legal issues in Islam. The fundamentalist view is that the Qur'an and Sunnah have provided guidance on all issues, while for example one modernist view expressed by Rahman (1979) is that social legislation is time specific and that the Qur'an mandates that humanity use reason.
7 Refer to http://hangingodes.wordpress.com/2006/11/10/revisiting-fazlur-rahmans-ordeal/ (weblog visited June 10, 2014).
8 There are many good accounts of the Zia era. Waseem (1987) is recommended here as a narrative by one of Pakistan's leading political scientists.
9 Mostly this is a declaration to the Prophet, while in some cases it is a statement by the Prophet.
10 This verse suggests that there is no need for *fatwas* (legal pronouncements) or militancy against anyone ridiculing Islam or its Prophet.
11 While we summarized the critique of conventional microcredit in this introduction to emphasize the importance of a research question, we have devoted Chapter 4 of this book to a full review of the critiques of microcredit and provided the documentation.
12 www.ppaf.org.pk/ (viewed June 7, 2014). Assuming an average household size of seven (Government of Pakistan, 1998), this level of credit outreach has national significance.
13 Khan, Rifaqat and Kazmi (2007, pp. 78–82).
14 Zaidi et. al. (2007).
15 Yunus (2002, p. 496).
16 www.povertyactionlab.org/.
17 The term 'sharing' could be appropriately used for what Akhuwat does. However, that term has been incorrectly appropriated to describe the likes of for-profit entities such as Uber and Airbnb. In the latter case, excess capacity is sold, but it does not represent income or wealth being shared, and that should be the hallmark of a true 'sharing economy.' A moral economy based on goodness, fairness and justice is another possibility. However, as conventionally defined, these are locally based economies based on mutuality. The key point of a 'giving economy,' as Akhuwat sees it, is that nothing is expected in exchange for the giving and free riding is not an issue.

References

Khan, S. R. 1987. *Profit and Loss Sharing: An Economic Analysis of an Islamic Financial System* (Karachi: Oxford University Press).
Khan, S. R., S. Kazmi and Z. Rifaqat. 2007. *Harnessing and Guiding Social Capital for Rural Development* (New York: Palgrave Macmillan).

Lindblom, C. 1977. *Politics and Markets: The World's Political Economic Systems* (New York: Basic Books).
Rahman, F. 1979. *Islam* (Chicago: University of Chicago Press), 2nd edition.
Waseem, M. 1987. *Pakistan Under Martial Law, 1977–1985* (Lahore, Pakistan: Vanguard Books).
Yunus, M. 2002. "Poverty Alleviation: Is Economics Any Help? Lessons from the Grameen Bank Experience," in P. Athukorala (ed.), *The Economic Development of South Asia* (Northampton, MA: Edward Elgar), pp. 487–505.
Zaidi, S. A., H. Jamal, S. Javeed and S. Zaka. 2007. "Social Impact Assessment of Microfinance Programmes," study commissioned by the European Union and Pakistan Financial Sector Reform Programme, Islamabad.

2 Altruism and faith-inspired giving[1]

Introduction

We explore altruism in this chapter since it is central to Akhuwat's modus operandi on the fund-raising and lending sides of its microcredit operations. In this chapter, we first explore the conceptual frameworks drawn from the economics literature that pertain to faith-inspired giving.[2] We turn next to how these apply to giving in Islam in general and Akhuwat in particular. We identify some practical issues of giving in Islam that emerge from the conceptual discussions and finally work towards a working definition of altruism that we refer back to in the empirical Chapters (6 and 7) and use it to evaluate Akhuwat's work.

Conceptual issues

A prominent conceptual approach in mainstream economics pertaining to faith-inspired giving includes utilitarianism that Becker (1981) extended to altruism within the family. Individuals have preferences that are assumed to be stable and consistent over time, and based on these they maximize utility subject to budget constraints. Altruism is not defined philosophically but rather in behavioral terms as interdependent utility functions.[3] Thus, within the household, the utility functions are positively associated with each other, and in this context giving within the family enhances the utility of the giver and the beneficiary (pp. 173–174). Giving within the family is consistent with utilitarianism in that the parents enhance their utility by enhancing that of their children. This suggests that pure egoism or self-interest is not a foundational principle of behavior, and in this regard utilitarianism is broader than egoism or self-interest.

Extending this framework to the broader society in the context of faith-inspired giving would mean individuals not only enhance their utilities by giving within the family but also beyond that to those less prosperous.

This broader interdependence can be traced back to the opening sentence of Smith's (2014) *Theory of Moral Sentiments*, which asserts: "How selfish so ever man may be supposed, there are evidently some principles in his nature, which interest him in the fortune of others, and render their happiness to him, though he derives nothing from it except the pleasure of seeing it." He ends the first paragraph by asserting that such compassion and empathy is not confined to the more virtuous or humane and that "[t]he greatest ruffian, the most hardened violator of the laws of society, is not altogether without it."

Smith's observation above suggests that humans are complex and multidimensional but most importantly that they exhibit empathy. For the moment, let us continue with a utilitarian perspective. Since faith-inspired giving is premised on seeking God's favor, the interdependence of utility functions is not needed. Utility in this case is derived merely from the act of giving and not necessarily from the knowledge that another's well-being has been enhanced. In the context of the broader economics literature on altruism, such giving would be referred to as impure altruism since a "warm glow" from giving cannot be ruled out (Zarri, 2013, p. 10).

Various economists have extended the household production/consumption utility maximization model to include religiosity including the pioneering work of Azzi and Ehrenberg (1975).[4] The novelty in the model is extending the framework to a multi-period utility maximization framework with afterlife consumption in the utility function. Afterlife consumption represents the reward from righteous living, including charitable giving, in the hereafter. They derive various hypotheses resulting from the model such as the substitution of charitable contributions for donated time based on the steepness of the age earning profile and use available data to test the hypotheses.

Sen's (1977) objection to such extensions of this utility-maximization framework was that as long as the preference order is consistent, this approach, particularly the revealed preference variant, is in accord with a whole range of human natures including that of a "single minded egoist or a raving altruist." Sen identified circularity in such methodological individualist economic theorizing based on rationality and self-interest. The starting point includes a consistent preference ordering based on specified axioms that lead to choices given budget constraints. However, preferences are not observable, and so they are therefore inferred from choices, explicitly so in the revealed preference framework (p. 325).

While Becker deliberately abstracted from motivation, the conception of human nature and hence motivation was of central concern for Sen since he viewed that to have a bearing on the kind of economic models that could be admitted into economic analysis (1977, p. 322). Sen introduced the concept of commitment whereby one is willing to do something for someone else because it is the right thing to do. In this case, utility functions are not interdependent. Sympathy, an alternative concept consistent with interdependent utility functions, may induce the same action but is egotistical in that the motivation is driven by feeling another's pain or pleasure (p. 326).

Commitment for Sen "drives a wedge between personal choice and personal welfare" (p. 329) as long as one, in his view, correctly understands preference to mean being better or worse off rather than simply choosing. This introduces the possibility of accepting human motivation other than egoism or utilitarianism in framing economic models. Morals, including those rooted in religion, could drive commitment. The practical relevance of this he pointed out pertains for example to the provision of public goods and also of understanding the role of morality and trust in collective action and the functioning of organizations such as Akhuwat (p. 331).

We do not view methodological individualism to be the only or even a reasonable framework for many economic issues. We also do not accept self-interest as the only motivation for individual action. However, we find it difficult to imagine a level of detachment such that doing the right thing does not also create a sense of well-being (referred to in the literature as warm glow as indicated previously – impure altruism). However, we accept Vernon Smith's critique that models framed in a utilitarian context may not capture the complexity of human behavior.

On EconTalk (April 6, 2015), Vernon Smith objected to including altruism in the utility function as an ex post hoc fit and hence as bad science.[5] He suggested that this amounted to first having observed how people behave and then inventing a utility function consistent with that. Proper theorizing would require such a utility function to emerge from modeling the dynamics of social interactions, and human codes of conduct or rules implicit in them (including those that are faith-inspired), with altruism resulting as a prediction from such functions.

Questions related to this critique are whether humans are hard wired to be a particular way, or do they respond to the environment they are born into, or can they be driven simultaneously by a whole range of complex motivations and observed behaviors including being empathetic and self-centered. Are they self-motivated because of the stimuli generated by capitalist market economies they are born into, or do neo-classical postulates accurately represent average human behavior and, following from that, key hypothesis like a downward sloping demand curve are not falsified, assuming one accepts methodological individualism and the scientific method as applicable to social sciences. Even if the latter was the case, we agree with Vernon Smith that it would be necessary to go back to first principles to capture the complexity of human behavior.

Applications to Islamic giving and Akhuwat

There are several forms of giving in Islam. The reference in this section is to *infaq* (voluntary giving). All references we have come across in the Qur'an to giving suggest it is an individual voluntary act, preferably anonymous, for spiritual growth (see below). The organization that is the recipient of the voluntary giving (*infaq*) can in turn provide *Qarz-e-Hassn* (literally beautiful loans). These are interest free, and the borrower pays back only the principal. This is precisely the approach to interest-free microcredit adopted by Akhuwat.[6]

However, Akhuwat's approach to microcredit is much broader since its founder, Amjad Saqib, derived inspiration from the *Mwakhaat-i-Medina* (brotherhood) during the origins of Islam as explained in the Preface. The incipient Muslim community in Mecca faced persecution and extermination in Mecca and hence migrated (*Hijra*) to Medina in 622 AD. The followers of the Prophet in Medina (*ansar*) adopted emigrants (*muhajirs*) until they could become self-sufficient. This is a parable for all times for Muslim regarding the spirit of social solidarity to aspire to.

Thus, the name Akhuwat encapsulates this spirit of *bhaichara*, or 'brotherhood.' More broadly, "social solidarity" and "empathy" are the social change the founder wants to bring about using microcredit as a tool. Humans in a capitalist market economy absorb stimuli to behave in self-interested ways, and Akhuwat is hence a mission to counter this by making them other conscious and to promote social solidarity.

To summarize, the principles of Akhuwat derived from *Mwakhaat-i-Medina* are giving a hand up and enabling borrowers to stand on their feet (Saqib, 2014, pp. 30–32). By using mosques, a collective community space, not only are overheads minimized, but the collective and social solidarity are emphasized. One key mechanism of worship in Islam is by serving the community, and so establishing and strengthening a relationship with God is both direct and indirect. Social solidarity rather than any punitive mechanism is the ideal to ensure repayment – just as individuals were helped, they are encouraged to perceive their repayment as a mechanism for helping others and continuing the good work.

In addition, the organization seeks to work with individuals through microcredit to make them self-sufficient and enable them to stand on their feet much as happened in early Islam with the migrants who found self-sufficiency through production and trade. The goal ultimately is that borrowers or recipients become givers.

The Qur'anic view of human nature is that humans are created in the "best of molds" and yet capable of descending to the "lowest of the low" (95:4). In a natural state, humans are viewed as weak (4:28) and avaricious

(17:100) and hence the need for spiritual striving including that embodied in giving. Adopting again a utilitarian perspective for now, if giving, income, goods or time is faith-inspired, then the positive feelings generated by such action must completely dominate the disutility, if any, of giving or engaging in good works at a point in time. This is because the reward for good works would presumably begin with the Hereafter and extend to infinity. Thus, no matter how high the disutility, it would be completely dwarfed by any perceived gains because these extend to infinity.[7]

This way of viewing action for believers raises some interesting questions. For example, could one view "good works" as a bribe? The answer is no because a probability of a positive return can be ascribed to a bribe, and faith in the Hereafter cannot be characterized in the same way. Could one view good works as insurance? Again, this would belie faith, and so the answer is no. In fact, for the pious, there may not be any disutility involved in engaging in good works. This raises another question. If there is no disutility from good works, there should be no limit to giving, and the pious should give all and perhaps live a hermitic existence doing good and waiting for the next life. Indeed the Qur'an views earthly life as merely "fleeting pleasure," "play," "sport," "amusement" or "diversion" (8:67, 9:38, 13:26, 16:94, 17:20, 29:64, 42:36, 47:36, 57:20, 75:20, 76:27).

However, Islam also enjoins on believers to assume the challenge of faith and good works while engaged in the hum drum of conventional existence and fully subject to life's temptations. Indeed, overcoming the temptations of normal existence is viewed as more challenging than being faithful while living a hermitic existence. Hence asceticism, withdrawal or the path of the hermit is not recommended (57:27).[8] Living a normal life then limits giving since individuals are subject to the constraint of fulfilling one's responsibility to the family and self. In addition, there is the Qur'anic injunction that giving should be guided by moderation so that one is "neither niggardly nor prodigal" (23:67).

Following from the above religious injunctions, there is a duality in the existence of a believing Islamic person.[9] At one level, as long as they are ethical (giving full measure and weight as enjoined on them [11:85, 17:35, 26:181–183], they are also urged to seek profit and prosper even as they remember the Creator's blessings. This aspect of behavior could be viewed as consistent with "homo economicus."[10] However, people are multi-dimensional and are also prone to giving others income, goods and time and hence denying self-consumption.[11]

We assume that faith-inspired giving induces a sense of well-being and that is sufficient motivation since no temporal reciprocity is expected from the giving. Indeed the best form of giving in Islam is one that is anonymous, such that neither the receiver nor the world should know of the giving so

Altruism and faith-inspired giving 19

that it is purely an expression of faith and doing what is prescribed (2:264, 2:271).[12] However, this motivation for giving obviates the need to assume interdependence of utility functions as indicated above. It may also create a social demand for faith-inspired organizations like Akhuwat as social intermediaries to channel funds.

Again, interdependence of utility functions plays no part in the process other than that the more prosperous are deemed to be tested by the less prosperous and vice versa or for mutual service (43:32). Agency belongs to God so the receiver's gratitude is to God. Faith-inspired organizations like Akhuwat, mediating donor (those who contribute to Akhuwat's credit pool), funds can only hope that the beneficiaries/borrowers will imbibe "the golden rule" and become future givers if they are successful and hence fulfill an obligation to God, the community and themselves.

In Hahn's (1991) terms, the benevolence at issue here is both named, since charity begins at home, but also unnamed or anonymous. Charity in Islam is due among others to the "wayfarers" and the poor in general (2:177, 2:215); in fact, it is also due to anyone who asks (93:10). Once again, the focus is on the giving and not on the receiving.

If average behavior was guided by these principles, Islamic societies would be utopian. For example, there would be few rapacious and predatory businesses, little corruption, and extensive charity. In practice, we know of no Islamic society that has been able to rely on a moral code to attain a good society. Thus, in practice, religiosity and practice based on that is no substitute for effectively enforced regulation and an earthly struggle to attain social justice. This is consistent with the Creator's understanding of his creation and the challenges humans confront for self and social improvement as indicated above. However, even if it will never be possible to dispense with state and community action to attain a good society in this world, many do internalize an ethical code of conduct in their own behavior and in the organizations they found. Our focus in this book is on studying one such organization.

Some practical issues pertaining to Islamic giving

In conventional giving, one might expect direct or indirect donor oversight. However, if the giving is faith-inspired, well-being is induced as earlier indicated by the giving and not from the knowledge that the giving has been effective.[13] The act of giving fulfils a moral responsibility and creates the sense of well-being. By contrast, Boulding (1973, p. 12) suggests that the motivation for giving in a secular framework might be based on the perception of efficiency of the grant or the extent of identification with the well-being of the recipient.[14]

If giving in and of itself dispenses the giver's responsibility, there is little incentive to giving wisely in terms of say optimizing the social returns to giving.[15] The practical importance of this aspect of giving is that public policy might need to be more vigilant to avoid scams. However, one would expect no "crowding out" as discussed in the literature since the giving is internally motivated by religiosity and not necessarily extrinsically motivated by the well-being of others, although both may be at play. In any case, more giving by some would not reduce the giving by others if religiosity is driving the giving.

A common understanding in Muslim societies is that religiosity increases as people age and come closer to the Day of Reckoning. If this is true, other things constant, age should have a positive association with giving.[16] Thus, demographics (aging population) would impact on the extent of overall giving, and there would be more pressure on the state to meet the basic needs of a younger population since average voluntary donations for welfare would be lower.

As Muslim states mature and strengthen their administrative capacity to deliver welfare, there would be less need for philanthropy though it might find other channels given the intrinsic motivation to engage in it. Exploring for example how giving can vary with demographics in such a framework could be useful for public policy. We also think that more oversight may be needed by the state if donors use intermediary civil society organizations like Akhuwat. This is again because donors motivated by religious commitment may focus more on the giving and less on the use of the funds.

Giving and a working definition of altruism[17]

Is giving for God altruism or maximizing behavior? Only the crudest Islamic teaching, where the Malvi (Mosque leader) quantifies merits earned and people believe this teaching, is entirely consistent with utility maximization. As earlier stated, we view humans to be multidimensional and motivations accordingly complex. Certainly the responses documented in Chapter 3 for Punjab and Sindh Provinces and those we recorded in our own survey responses (Chapter 6) to the question of "why do you give" confirmed this view.

Giving could be based on a whole array of factors not necessarily independent of each other such as empathy or social solidarity based on humanistic beliefs, winning God's favor and earning merits, attaining a "warm glow," social pressure or social recognition. In the latter case, such recognition of a good citizen status may also result in material benefits such as a "philanthropic" car dealer getting more business. Akhuwat emphasizes giving so that others can benefit, and this view was echoed by borrowers (see Chapter 6). Only in a few cases did borrowers speculate that perhaps getting another loan might be conditional on their current generosity which is recorded and public.

One can argue that the altruism based on humanistic philosophy is the purist form of giving since there is absolutely no ulterior motive for the giving and there is no expectation of a return in this life or the next (pure altruism). Wilson (2015, p. 3) defines such altruism as "concern for others as an end in itself." This echoes Smith's empathy and Sen's concept of commitment.

An alternative working definition of altruism is when people contribute to the material well-being of others without any guarantee of a *material* reward for themselves as a *consequence*, direct or indirect, of that contribution. The emphasis is on the word material as well as on the lack of causal consequence between the act of giving and any guaranteed future material gain. Akhuwat's vision is to turn borrowers into altruistic donors. A minimum condition for this to be realized is that donors, particularly those with an ongoing association with the organization, make their contributions anonymously. For example, if this condition does not hold, they may well be making their donations with an ulterior motive of seeking a loan renewal.

If we thus define altruism, then giving because of celestial reward could still be consistent with altruism. There is a qualitative difference in an ulterior motive where the temporal material return has a very high probability compared to a spiritual return which is premised on faith, and therefore one could argue that there is no "guaranteed" future gain even if those with faith believe there is.[18]

Giving now in response to having received in the past would also be consistent with altruism especially if the eventual receiver is independent of the original giver. Altruism could be based on social convention or an individualistic value system. However, if social conventions are derived from religious interpretations (narrow or broad), the distinction may be difficult to make since the two are so intertwined.

We are restricting ourselves to material contributions and rewards as economists since the subject is largely about material transactions. Further, and more importantly, if there is evidence of widespread altruism in line with the more restrictive (second) definition, it can help with the understanding of issues like trust and cooperation in a wider social context than the one on which standard two-agent game theoretic rationalization is based.

Summary and conclusions

We think a whole range of human behavior is possible and taking an absolutist stance one way or the other is not warranted. Further, we think human behavior is dynamic and not static and can change even over the course of one's life from self-interested to altruistic. This is implicitly Akhuwat's presumption, and its mission to create social solidarity and empathy through its microcredit and other philanthropic interventions follow from this presumption.

One could argue that such an endeavor should be supported by evidence on human behavior. Our view is that well-designed empirical experiments can at best capture average human behavior at a point in time, whereas Akhuwat's concern is with changing human behavior over time. Attempting to capture such change empirically might be possible in an extremely expensive panel study but likely to be subject to many design flaws.[19]

In this chapter, we explore the economics literature to understand altruism. We rule out the utility maximizing framework based on the Sen and Vernon circularity critiques. This framework is also deemed inadequate to analyze giving in a faith-inspired context given the multidimensionality of human behavior and the ensuing complexity of motivations. Thus, using neoclassical behavioral postulates to theorize about and understand altruistic behavior, in a society where citizens have internalized a faith-inspired code of conduct in business or in doing good works, is not attempted.[20]

We argue instead that Smith's and Sen's view of empathy and commitment is closer to an understanding of altruistic motivation in the Islamic tradition. However, compared to the humanitarian tradition of pure altruism based on commitment, faith-inspired giving could be viewed as driven by an ulterior motive and hence impure altruism. We argue that because there is no objective certainty of a reward and because the reward, even if anticipated, is not material, giving motivated by a celestial reward is still altruism. However, we argue that a minimum condition for such altruism is that the giving be anonymous.

This is the working definition of altruism that Akhuwat is expected to rely on for its interest-free microcredit and its non-microcredit philanthropic initiatives. We explore the latter in Chapter 3 and then move on in the rest of the book to explore its microcredit initiative. We refer back to this working definition of altruism in evaluating Akhuwat's policy in a microcredit context of converting borrowers into donors to realize its vision of *bhaichara* or empathy and social solidarity.

Notes

1 Faith-inspired is distinguished from faith-based to emphasize its multi and inter dimensional nature – i.e. the inspiration is not derived from any particular religion or sect/denomination within a religion. This distinction was suggested by Fatima Rasheed.
2 Refer to Wilson (2015) for an evolutionary perspective. His take in Chapter 7 on the economist perspective from this vantage point is particularly interesting.

Altruism and faith-inspired giving 23

3 This is implicit in Becker's "rotten kid theorem."
4 Schwartz (1970) earlier utilized the utility maximizing model to explore philanthropic giving.
5 http://www.econtalk.org/archives/2014/11/vernon_smith_on_2.html. This is similar to the circularity referred to by Sen.
6 Other forms of giving – including *sadaqa*, *khums*, *kuffarah*, *fitrah* and *nazr* – are purpose based and hence different.
7 One could conceive of a high enough discount rate at which this is not the case, but faith presupposes a low if not zero discount rate.
8 Also see "Verses of the Quran that Define Society." www.islamicity.org/forum/forum_posts.asp?TID=32663 (consulted November 28, 2017).
9 This is similar to the human duality Sen (1987, p. 41) referred to, although the context is different.
10 For those who consider themselves Muslim, profit maximizing is constrained by a Qur'anic moral code, while for others it may be constrained by a moral code derived from other religions or a personal code of ethics.
11 Many experimental economics studies on altruism suggest this to be the case. Refer for example to Ottoni-Wilhelm, Vesterlund, and Xie (2014).
12 Further, since the Qur'an (3:92) enjoins the spending "from that which people love," this would include time which for many is more difficult to part with.
13 This conjecture may be borne out in survey responses documented in a study on philanthropy in Pakistan (see Chapter 3, Bonbright and Azfar, 2000). For example, over half (56 percent) did not express an interest in the actual use of the grants (p. 59), and only two-fifths cared about the contribution making a difference. However, this finding is contradicted by the Islamic tradition of personal giving, and so for example 71 percent in Punjab Province preferred to give to individuals themselves rather than indirectly via an organization. Also refer to Thorton and Helms (2013) and Wen-Chun (2005) on the religious motivation for giving in other contexts.
14 Also refer to Zarri (2013) on the motivations for giving including self-esteem.
15 Once again, this is clearly evident in giving behavior in Pakistan (refer to Chapter 3).
16 This effect has been empirically shown by Azzi and Ehrenberg (1975), Ehrenberg (1977), Iannaccone (1998) and Hrung (2004).
17 Saqib Jafarey, Professor of Economics, City University, contributed generously to this section.
18 Clearly the stronger the faith, the higher the perceived probability of a return, but no one other than God can know the strength of faith.
19 Refer to Appendix 7.1 for potential design flaws in a much less ambitious study.
20 For the limitations of a neo-classical approach and ways of moving beyond methodological individualism, refer to Collard (1978), Sen (1987) and Basu (2010).

References

Azzi, C. and R. G. Ehrenberg. 1975. "Household Allocation of Time and Church Attendance," *Journal of Political Economy*, 83(1), 27–546.
Basu, K. 2010. *Beyond the Invisible Hand: Groundwork for a New Economics* (Princeton: Princeton University Press).

Becker, G. 1981. *A Treatise on the Family* (Cambridge, MA: Harvard University Press).
Bonbright, D and A. Azfar. 2000. "Philanthropy in Pakistan: A Report of the Initiative on Indigenous Philanthropy" (np: Aga Khan Foundation).
Boulding, K. 1973. *The Economy of Love and Fear: A Preface to Grants Economics* (Belmont, CA: Wadsworth Publishing Company, Inc.).
Chang, Wen-Chun. 2005. "Religious Giving, Non-Religious Giving, and After-Life Consumption," *B. E. Journal of Economic Analysis and Policy: Topics in Economic Analysis*, 5(1), 1–31.
Collard, D. A. 1978. *Altruism and Economy: A Study of Non-Selfish Economics* (New York: Oxford University Press).
Ehrenberg, R. G. 1977. "Household Application of Time and Religiosity: Replication and Extension," *Journal of Political Economy*, 85(2), 415–423.
Hahn, F. 1991. "Benevolence," in G. Meeks (ed.), *Thoughtful Economic Man: Essays on Rationality, Moral Rules and Benevolence* (Cambridge: Cambridge University Press).
Hrung, W. B. 2004. "After-Life Consumption and Charitable Giving," *American Journal of Economics and Sociology*, 63(3), 731–745.
Iannaccone, L. R. 1998. "Introduction to the Economics of Religion," *Journal of Economic Literature*, 36(3), 1465–1496.
Ottoni-Wilhelm, M., L. Vesterlund and H. Xie. 2014. "Why Do People Give? Testing Pure and Impure Altruism," NBER Working Paper No. 20497, National Bureau of Economic Research, Cambridge, MA, www.nber.org/papers/w20497.
Saqib, A. 2014. *Akhuwat ka Safar* (Lahore: Sang-e-Meel).
Schwartz, R. A. 1970. "Personal Philanthropic Contributions," *Journal of Political Economy*, 78(6), 1264–1291.
Sen, A. K. 1987. *On Ethics and Economics* (Cambridge, MA: Basil Blackwell).
Sen, A. K. 1977. "Rational Fools: A Critique of the Behavioral Foundations of Economic Theory," *Philosophy & Public Affairs*, 6(4), 317–344.
Smith, A. 2014. *The Theory of Moral Sentiments* (San Bernardino, CA: Amazon).
Thorton, J. P. and S. Helms. 2013. "Afterlife Incentives in Charitable Giving," *Applied Economics*, 45(19–21), 2279–2291.
Wilson, D. S. 2015. *Does Altruism Exist: Culture, Genes, and the Welfare of Others* (New Haven: Yale University Press).
Zarri, L. 2013. "Altruism," in S. B. Zamagni and F. A. Luigino (eds.), *Handbook on the Economics of Reciprocity and Social Enterprise* (Northampton, MA: Edward Elgar).

3 Altruism in Pakistan and Akhuwat's altruistic initiatives

Introduction

This chapter starts with a review of altruism in Pakistan and in that context reviews Akhuwat's initiatives next. While there is a distinction between organizational altruism, such as that of Akhuwat's, and that driven by individual initiative, the distinction is not hard and fast. Individual altruism often drives organizational altruism, while organizational altruism can be the embodiment of an individual's vision. In Akhuwat's case, Dr. Amjad Saqib's vision and energy, with full support from the Board of Governors, is driving several initiatives other than microcredit.

Philanthropy in Pakistan

Philanthropic giving and civil society engagement in Pakistan is well established and started becoming institutionalized under British rule with the Societies Act, 1860, and Trust Act, 1882. More recent legislation includes the Voluntary Social Welfare Agencies Ordinance, 1961, and the Companies Act, 1984. There are over a hundred apex intermediary organizations providing social services through a network of grassroots groups, and Akhuwat (registered under the Societies Act, 1860) counts among them.

Chapter 4 of the report by Bonbright and Azfar (2000) drew on work commissioned by Aga Khan Foundation to Arshad Zaman Associates on dimensions of individual giving (time, money, goods). The reference here is to non-obligatory giving which the donors may consider *infaq* (see Chapter 2). This study reported results based on a household survey which replicated three studies done in the United States, adapting it for social and cultural differences. The survey instrument contained 142 questions, and the respondents were selected based on a two-stage stratified random sample with 1,365 (390 females) individuals responding. The margin of error on statistics was reported to be plus or minus 3 percent.

26 Conceptual and institutional issues

By blowing up the numbers based on the sample survey, the study concluded that aggregate giving in Pakistan in 1998 amounted to Rs. 70.5 billion (p. 59). For perspective, this amounted to 2.2 percent of GDP (p. 88), close to the combined average government expenditure on health and education in 1996–1997, and about five times the amount received in foreign grant aid (p. 59).

Ninety-eight percent of the donors cited religious faith as a motivation for giving, and much (two-thirds) of it was to individuals based on expressed need as was the case for volunteering time (two-fifths). Over half (56 percent) did not express an interest in the actual use of the grants (p. 59), and only two-fifths cared about the contribution making a difference. Only 11 percent agreed that giving was for acquiring social approval or status, and only 15 percent had a tax motivation (pp. 72–73).

The Pakistan Center for Philanthropy (2012) has commissioned several reports since the above benchmark study using the latter as a frame of reference. Using a similar stratified two-stage sampling design to reach a representative sample, it interviewed 2,000 households in the Punjab, Pakistan's most populous province, in 2010. Table 4.11 (p. 24) documented reasons for giving and hence is particularly interesting from our perspective. Returning something to society, citizen responsibility, compassion, faith and social obligation were mentioned by four-fifths or more as reasons for giving. Enhancing status or tax deduction was rated as reasons by about a tenth of the respondents. Another interesting finding is that at least 84 percent of all giving came from individuals making an income of Rs. 20,000 or less, i.e. lower middle class or less prosperous (Nayab, 2011).

In a follow-up study by the Community Development Program, Government of Sindh and the Pakistan Center of Philanthropy (2015), the state of philanthropy in Sindh, Pakistan's second-most populous province, was explored. Once again a two-stage stratified random sample was used to select a representative sample of 3,000 households. Ninety-seven percent of households engaged in some form of giving. Also, the main motivations for giving once again were religion (94 percent) and human compassion (92 percent). Only 5 percent responded that tax deduction or acquiring status was a motivation (p. 34).[1]

Bonbright and Afzar attempt to provide a global context for Pakistani charitable giving. By comparing survey results to comparative international statistics, the authors concluded that Pakistan is among the most giving nations in the world (p. 88). The study constructed a National Index for Community Engagement (NICE) and compared scores of the United States and Pakistan. Overall, Pakistan's score of 53 (maximum 100) compared favorably to 42 for the United States, and the largest difference in the sub-components was 71 for spirit of voluntarism for Pakistan compared to 26 percent for the United States (p. 77). Fifty-eight percent of the respondents claimed to volunteer, and this was more than twice the global average (p. 58).

More recent evidence does not show Pakistan to be exceptional in civic engagement. For its 2016 Global Civic Engagement Report, Gallup (2016) asked 145,000 people in 140 countries in 2015 about their donations of money, time or assistance to a stranger. Myanmar topped the country ranking with a score of 70, with the United States coming in second with a score of 61. Pakistan, with a score of 29, ranked 60th out of the 140 nations ranked. Similarly, the Charities Aid Foundation (CAF) annually releases the World Giving Index based on helping a stranger, donating money and volunteering time. The CAF World Giving Index 2017 (2017) included 139 countries, and Pakistan ranked 78th. Notwithstanding Pakistan's disappointing comparative global ranking in altruism, Akhuwat is showing the way.

Akhuwat's altruistic initiatives[2]

Akhuwat views microcredit not as an all-encompassing solution to poverty alleviation, but rather as one element in attaining a supportive, socially inclusive, value infused society. As a result of this vision, it has also developed various additional initiatives, in addition to its flagship microcredit scheme, to work towards its objectives. These initiatives include minimizing waste, redistributing shared prosperity efficiently, productively mobilizing social resources and institutionalizing social solidarity.

They have established a Transgender Rehabilitation Program and have also supported Rabtt, launched by two former employees, which is an initiative to enhance critical thinking skills in society via workshops for children. Its broader community development programs include Akhuwat Health Services, Akhuwat Educational Assistance Program, Akhuwat University, Akhuwat Clothes Bank and Akhuwat Internship Program (part of the Akhuwat Institute of Social Enterprise Management). We describe below Akhuwat's charitable programs and initiatives.

Khwaja Sira Rehabilitation Program

The stigma associated with the third gender, or *khwaja siras* as they are known in Pakistan, has prohibited efforts towards their social and economic inclusion via support structures. In collaboration with Fountain House, Akhuwat launched a Transgender Rehabilitation Program in 2010 for older *khwaja siras* (50 plus). More recently, it also aims to help younger *khwaja siras* "through community awareness, encouraging a dialogue and by providing dignified skill development and livelihood opportunities." The intervention focuses on removing the barriers that have led to the social and economic exclusion of the *khwaja sira* community.

The Transgender Rehabilitation Program came in to being when Gogi from the *khwaja sira* community visited Akhuwat's office at the Shah Jamal Mosque to convince Akhuwat staff to help her community (Rasheed and Ali, 2013). Gogi had been active in her pursuit for transgender rights for many years and made several visits in her struggle to courts, press clubs, offices and hospitals. This visit gave birth to what later came to be known as the Akhuwat *Khwaja Sira* Socio-Economic Rehabilitation Program. Gogi herself is now the Program Coordinator for the initiative.

After initially consulting with the *khwaja sira* community, it was realized that the simple extension of interest-free microcredit would not be sufficient to alleviate the plight of this community. Akhuwat ascertained that a broader development strategy was needed. In collaboration with Fountain House, it launched a multi-dimensional program to support the *khwaja siras* socially and emotionally. The program was designed in consultation with members of the *khwaja sira* community who later also emerged as spokespersons and local mobilizers for the project. The premises and facilities at Fountain House – including psychologists and social workers, rehabilitation programs, and skill-training units – were utilized to launch the program.

After the initial effort to build connections with the *khwaja sira* community, Akhuwat now relies on registered *khwaja siras* to introduce more members to the program. Through its peer-based outreach program, Akhuwat is able to reach out to more vulnerable individuals, while also empowering local members of the *khwaja sira* community to play a more proactive role in the development of their community.

Vulnerable *khwaja siras* are identified on the basis of age, economic isolation and the lack of access to social networks, and they are registered for a monthly stipend. This stipend, which serves as a gesture of goodwill, is allocated from solicited donations. It is provided with the intention of bringing some economic relief to the *khwaja siras* who due to extreme social and economic exclusion are unable to afford basic necessities. However the stipend size itself at Rs. 1,150 per month is quite negligible, and, while it can help provide immediate relief, it is debatable to what degree it can actually help 'rehabilitate' them.[3] Akhuwat's primary focus has been on older *khwaja siras* who find self-support more difficult. Akhuwat is also developing programs to offer skill trainings and interest-free micro-finance to make the community financially self-sufficient.

Under the program, registered *khwaja siras* are provided with basic healthcare facilities through Akhuwat Health Services, including routine medical check-ups, diagnostic facilities and medicines, and treatment of chronic illnesses. Members are issued health cards so that they may access quality subsidized health services from different medical centers and professionals. During each month's gathering, qualified professionals give seminars on the fundamentals of hygiene, nutrition and prevention of diseases, with a special focus on hepatitis, HIV/AIDS and other sexually transmitted diseases (STDs).

Social exclusion and prejudice against *khwaja siras* is manifested in years of emotional and physical violence. For this reason, psychologists and psychiatrists available at Fountain House have been made accessible on a regular basis for this program to help *khwaja siras* overcome emotional distress, depression, anxiety and other psychological disorders.[4]

The facilities of Fountain House are used for a half-day long event on the 15th of each month which includes the disbursement of funds, entertainment, exchange of gifts and lunch. Members of civil society are invited and attending *khwaja siras* are provided mentoring on a wide range of topics including health, ethics and religion. These gatherings are viewed successful in fostering dialogue and contributing to a mutual understanding and respect between *khwaja siras* and other members of society.

Akhuwat's website notes that its main interest in establishing an income support mechanism for the transgendered is to be able to create a social support network. The idea is that such individuals can feel part of a collective, have an opportunity to share their burdens and distress, and be treated with compassion. In essence, Akhuwat aims to reinforce their self-esteem with emotional support, mentoring and advice. This proves valuable, especially in a patriarchal and increasingly polarized society like Pakistan, where gender and gender roles are also religiously mandated and negotiating them is not easy.

One ugly incident was religious posters in some urban shopping areas in Pakistan's largest city (Karachi) claiming that "*khwaja siras* are in fact men disguised as women" and that "they would be beheaded in Saudi Arabia for their transgressions," but this did not happen in Pakistan because it has a weak state (Hasan, 2016). Given this oppressive social context the *khwaja sira* community faces, Akhuwat's support is commendable.

With the expansion of the programs, many *khwaja siras* expressed the desire to develop basic literacy skills. In collaboration with Fountain House, a literacy program has been initiated to impart basic reading, numeracy, arithmetic and writing skills for those unable to pursue their education.

The major thrust of the programs is to assist *khwaja siras* in acquiring sustainable livelihoods and remove their dependency on alms. Complemented with efforts aimed at social integration, it is envisioned that their financial empowerment will translate into social inclusion and self-sufficiency. For this reason, a number of services are being offered to the *khwaja sira* community as explained above so that they may create their own pathway out of poverty.[5]

30 Conceptual and institutional issues

Akhuwat has employed seven *khwaja siras* to manage its Clothes Bank Program (see below) based in its head office. Not only is Akhuwat focusing on them as beneficiaries or "target recipients," but it has integrated them as part of its own organizational processes, thus representing its commitment to true socioeconomic inclusion being realized, notwithstanding the small number hired.

Through the continued support from donors and volunteers, Akhuwat has been able to expand the program, reaching out to residents in Lahore and surrounding areas. Through the increase in Akhuwat's volunteer base and proactive involvement of civil society, it has been able to provide several services to create a more extensive support system for members. It has plans to expand operations beyond Lahore to other cities of Pakistan.

As of August 2017, 695 *khwaja siras* were registered, and 482 were receiving monthly stipends of Rs. 1,150.[6] In addition, they deposit Rs. 50 every month as a contingency fund for emergencies. Three hundred therapy sessions, 96 health camps and three trainings had been conducted on their behalf with one *khwaja sira* qualifying as a beautician. Ten had been provided with regular employment (three at Fountain House, four at the Clothes Bank and three elsewhere in the organization).

As a large faith-inspired organization, Akhuwat's validation of the third gender through its programs is highly commendable. However their validation needs to be rooted in social justice and mutuality rather than in patronizing notions of morality and respectability, which can often be a risk with faith-based initiatives.

Akhuwat Clothes Bank

The Clothes Bank initiative was launched in 2014 to extend Akhuwat's microcredit program to a non-monetary space. Thus, the well-off are encouraged to donate unneeded clothes to the organization so that it can productively donate them to those who need them after washing and packaging.

As of August 2017, Akhuwat Clothes Bank had disbursed 1,550,000 articles of clothing from its three disbursement centers in Lahore, Karachi and Rawalpindi with a current monthly disbursement rate of 70,000. Dewar-e-Akhuwat (*dewar* means wall) is a new initiative to extend the work of the Clothes Bank. Outside many of the 500 branches of Akhuwat, a wall has been reserved on which abandoned, repaired and cleaned clothes are hung for poverty-stricken individuals. This plan is also implemented outside Akhuwat schools (see below).

Akhuwat has launched a Book Bank Program to serve underprivileged communities and had 150 book corners under development and six libraries established by mid-2016. It has also started a Food Bank designed to provide meals to needy families. It aims to curtail the enormous wastage of food from marriage halls and food outlets by collecting excess edibles at the end of the day to distribute amongst impoverished communities.

Rabtt[7]

Akhuwat's emphasis on solidarity and volunteerism inspired and facilitated two of its former employees (Aneeq Cheema and Imran Sarwar) to develop an education venture premised on building empathy and critical thinking in an organic and personalized way. The initiative aims to utilize empty school infrastructure in and around Lahore during the summer holiday months (similar to Akhuwat's productively operating through underutilized community spaces such as mosques and churches, see Chapter 5) to hold educational workshops and camps geared towards critical thinking. This is done by attempting to dissolve class, sectarian and ethnic barriers by recruiting university students and providing them an avenue to connect with less-privileged government school students via the classroom.

In a society like Pakistan – where class, sectarian and ethnic fissures divide the social fabric, and religious extremism permeates society – educational attainment is not only low[8] but also in constant threat of being hijacked by political agendas due to rising extremism and polarization. In this context, initiatives like Rabtt have an important role.[9]

The students at government schools that generally cater to students from low-income backgrounds (who otherwise do not normally have access to a stimulating curriculum that engages and empowers them to question and think critically) are taught courses like history, public speaking, art and dramatics in a hands-on and personalized setting. This encourages self-confidence and harnessing self-worth in citizenry, another core feature of Akhuwat's ideology. Furthermore, this also enhances the intellectual capital of the teachers. Through this process, Rabtt attempts to address the lack of quality education in public schools, compared to private schools, by supplementing the one-dimensional curriculum and impersonal classroom setting, with workshops and camps. As of October 15, 2016, they had held 30 summer camps and numerous workshops, engaging over 2,800 students and 300 mentors.[10]

Aneeq and Imran's commitment[11] to building an initiative around empathy is testament to Akhuwat's commitment to creating and instilling a value-driven culture of solidarity within and outside the organization.[12] Akhuwat's organizational culture is designed to promote selflessness, a sense of morality and volunteerism. The notion of "self-monitoring," which is an essential institutional characteristic for effective civil society organization and public institutions for development (Basu, 2010, p. 118), is derived from such altruism. Aneeq and Imran's motivation to start Rabtt as Akhuwat employees can be interpreted as an indication of this altruism, and an example of it being embodied and transmitted beyond Akhuwat as well. Both remain closely affiliated with Akhuwat as volunteers and often deliver talks for Akhuwat's Internship Program.

Akhuwat continues to provide advisory and financial support to Rabtt. At a foundational level, this also represents Akhuwat's commitment to human potential being realized (Sen, 1977), rather than encouraging skill development for the sole purpose of integration as economic agents in a market economy as is often the case with conventional micro-finance organizations.

Akhuwat Educational Assistance Program

Akhuwat provides an education loan in order to cater to the needs of those who are unable to finance their own or their children's education. The emphasis on education has been a central part of Akhuwat's social agenda since education can mean the realization of an individual's full potential. Apart from being able to engage productively in the economy, it can also enhance civic participation. In most cases, the education loan is utilized for paying fees and dues, purchasing books and material, and paying initial registration or examination fee. The upper limit of the education loans is Rs. 25,000, and as of January 2015, 101 scholars had been assisted (18 females). In addition, between March 23 and May 30, 2015, four sessions were held utilizing 22 resource persons to help 65 individuals with their mathematics skills.

It is currently running 302 schools for the poor in Jhang and Faisalabad districts of the Punjab province. This is a public-civil society partnership, and the plan was to make non-performing public schools functional under the Punjab Government's Public Schools Support Program. To date, 37,000 students have benefited from this education initiative. Akhuwat plans to adopt another 300–400 schools in the less developed areas of Pakistan.[13]

It is also partnering with a prominent education NGO, the Kiran Foundation, to take over non-performing government schools (two so far) in Lyari, a poor area of Karachi, as a public-civil society partnership to turn it into an inspiring "model" school for replication elsewhere. A novel feature is a pre-school with innovative learning involving over a hundred pre-school children and their mothers.

To further the cause of inclusive and accessible education, Akhuwat is also currently planning an Akhuwat University to be based in Lahore. It intends to offer merit based placement to 90 percent of deserving admits who will be encouraged to voluntarily repay their tuition costs once they are in a position to be able to do so. This is similar to its principle of borrowers-to-donors which it emphasizes in its microcredit program (see Chapter 5).

The fundraising for the university are currently underway and it is expected to be operational by 2018.[14]

Akhuwat Health Services (AHS)

As part of its loan products, Akhuwat instituted a health loan for those unable to afford necessary health care. In a low-middle income country like Pakistan, preventable and curable diseases (i.e. hepatitis, tuberculosis and diabetes) are common and often known to be fatal due to a lack of affordable treatment. In most cases, low-income households are unable to save contingency funds for circumstances like these. Thus a health loan was specifically designed to assist the poor with funds for treatment in the event of a contingency. The loans vary from Rs.10, 000 to Rs. 20,000. Since many of these diseases are also preventable with adequate awareness of precaution and hygiene, Akhuwat formally established the Akhuwat Health Services initiative as a subsidiary of their Microcredit Program.

AHS provides affordable and efficient health care service for underserved people, in addition to creating awareness. Based on prevention, cure and rehabilitation, the focus is on providing health facilities for low to middle income communities through the launch of camps, medical centers, and mobile clinics. It engages in proactive collaboration with partner health service providers to attain its objectives.

The Diabetes Center (AHS-DC) sponsors diabetes education and is directed towards preventative care as well as management of bodily complications emerging from the disease. The clinic conducts free sugar camps, filter clinics and awareness campaigns. Data concerning diabetic patients is accumulated to promote research and development in diabetic management. The patients are offered advice and expert instruction by well-known consultants with a 70 percent subsidy relative to market prices. As of August 31, 2017, 78,989 patients had received free treatment at the clinic.

The Gynae Clinic provides reproductive health services to women from low-income communities. The women are provided with examinations and consulting services along with health education and preventative care. Various forms of assistance are offered to foster understanding of self-care and assist the women to live informed and healthy life styles. As of August 31, 2017, 18,126 patients had been treated free of cost.

Akhuwat Dreams Project

Beginning in 2008, Akhuwat Dreams Project was initiated to fulfill the 'dreams' of children suffering from terminal illnesses. Dedicated play rooms in hospitals were established to offer bright, positive and playful environments for such children. The intention is to provide joyful distraction and give these children relief from the otherwise drab and serious hospital environments. By mid-2017, four rooms for this purpose had been established, 711 wishes had been met and 6,072 gifts distributed on Eid (Islam's holy holiday).

Conclusion

Akhuwat is often referred to as a social enterprise. If social enterprises are defined as those that are willing to forsake some profit to meet a social need, then this is a mischaracterization. Akhuwat certainly meets a social need, but it does so as a philanthropic organization. While its mission is purely characterized by altruism, it is a conduit of philanthropy since it uses donated funds to do 'good works' such as the initiatives reviewed in this chapter. The bulk of its 'good works' are the interest-free loans it provides to the poor based mainly on term grants that draw on its credit pool for on-lending. This is the activity we explore in the rest of this book.

In our view, philanthropic organizations like Akhuwat epitomize a crucial part of a 'giving economy' in societies were charity is enjoined on individuals by their faith. Individual charitable acts constitute another element of a giving economy. However, we see these elements as complementary in creating a giving economy. Ultimately, in our view as mentioned in Chapter 1, a giving society is one whereby the state is also used as a conduit via the tax/expenditure mechanism to ensure social well-being.

Akhuwat's engagement with the transgender community is interesting and a case-study on the question of gender engagement within a religious framework. Akhuwat seems to genuinely care and support the most disadvantaged, most notably the *khwaja sira* community, and its initiatives in this regard are welcome. However, Akhuwat operates in a patriarchal context wedded to existing respectability politics and hierarchies. Thus, while in the short run band-aid solutions are welcome, in the long run a state that redresses the structural causes of poverty, inequality and marginalization is the goal to strive for.

Notes

1 Our concern in this book is with individual giving. The Pakistan Centre of Philanthropy (2015) has also researched corporate philanthropy. The total amount given in 2000 (Rs 200 million) was 0.3 percent of the total amount contributed by individuals in 1999. Also the base is narrow with the top five public limited companies contributing over half the total contributions in 2014.
2 Information reported in this section is based on cited sources or interviews with Akhuwat head office personal or is drawn from the Akhuwat website. As

evident from its website, Akhuwat has diversified into activities, some mentioned in Chapter 1, other than those we have documented in this chapter. These include Akhuwat Faisalabad Institute of Research, Science and Technology (FIRST), Akhuwat Institute of Social Enterprise and Management (for training), Akhuwat Leadership and Fellowship Program (a four-week module to sensitize students to various organizations in the development sector). As of mid-2016, it had trained 1,150 fellows and interns at the rate of 60 per year. In 2017 it planned to train 350 interns from across nine cities across the country. Akhuwat's My Biz Incubator Center is designed to incubate micro enterprises, provide angel investment and build their capacity. It plans to scale up the pilot project to cater to 500 enterprises. Akhuwat Volunteer Services has created a network of volunteers among students and professionals and exposes them to disaster management, capacity building and event management and encourages them to undertake projects on their own.

3 We solicited feedback from an anthropology researcher, Mehlab Jameel, who identifies as trans and is a social justice activist in Lahore. Given the complete lack of support for this community and the marginalization and violence it faces on a daily basis, she was not dismissive of Akhuwat's support, but did wonder to what extent Akhuwat managed to 'rehabilitate' *khwaja siras* with a negligibly small monthly stipend. She noted that one Akhuwat therapist indicated a view of the community as "mired in socially deviant life styles and in need of rehabilitation" during one of the sessions. This raised the question for her of *what* exactly was being rehabilitated. While the program "reeks of a savior complex," she noted that unlike others, Akhuwat personnel are at the bare minimum not rude or unkind and that quite a few members of the *khwaja sira* community appreciate the program. However, problematic assumptions about 'respectability' and 'productivity' are reinforced under the guise of 'rehabilitation,' thus reinforcing structural hierarchies instead of challenging them.

4 We are not aware of the quality of services rendered. One of us attended a session in 2012, but at the time was not fully aware of the debates within which the session could be contextualized.

5 Setting up a small business is much easier than sustaining it amidst a daily onslaught of transphobic violence which quickly results in the loss of hope. To make these endeavors a success, Akhuwat would have to combat traditional notions of respectability in the communities that they serve. While that is a 'big ask,' it is probably only possible for an organization like Akhuwat because it has a large reservoir of goodwill and because it routinely challenges convention to emphasize decency and a common humanity' (see Chapter 8).

6 Due to death or movement, 192 files had been closed.

7 For more on Rabtt, see http://rabtt.org/#.

8 The overall literacy rate for 2016–2017 was reported by the *Pakistan Economic Survey*, Government of Pakistan, to be 58 percent while the 2016 Population Census, which made the definition of literacy more stringent, reported a literacy rate of 69 percent for men and 45 percent for women.

9 The Taliban attack on Malala Yusufzai in 2012 and the Peshawar attack on an Army Public School in 2014, which resulted in the massacre of 140 students, and fundamentalist attempts to hijack the curricula are examples of the threat to education in Pakistan.

10 Rabtt's website. On April 2017 they announced that the organization is suspending operations due to sustainability issues.

11 Sen's notion of "commitment" discussed in Chapter 2 applies here.
12 In an email exchange with one of us, Imran Sarwar stated: "At Rabtt we believe that any meaningful change in someone's life can only be brought about by establishing a close connection, a bond, with the other person – that we truly need to understand and empathize with each other to be able to move forward – and this philosophy has its roots in Akhuwat's message of brotherhood and solidarity."
13 Since public schools serve the poorest who cannot afford private schools, Akhuwat's managerial ability is serving a good cause. However, it terms of the larger picture, we object to such abdication of public responsibility to the private sector or civil society.
14 Information provided by Akhuwat head office.

References

Basu, K. 2010. *Beyond the Invisible Hand: Groundwork for a New Economics* (Princeton: Princeton University Press).

Bonbright, D. and A. Azfar. 2000. *Philanthropy in Pakistan: A Report of the Initiative on Indigenous Philanthropy* (np: Aga Khan Foundation).

Charity Aid Foundation. 2017. "CAF World Giving Index 2017: A Global View of Giving Trends," www.cafonline.org/docs/default-source/about-us-publications/cafworldgivingindex2017_2167a_web_040917.pdf.

Community Development Program, Government of Sindh and Pakistan Center for Philanthropy. 2015. "Individual Indigenous Philanthropy in Sindh," Islamabad.

Gallup. 2016. "Global Civic Engagement Report 2016," www.gallup.com/topic/report.aspx.

Hasan, F. 2016. "Posters Calling for 'Beheading' Transwomen Surface on Tariq Road," The Express Tribune, Karachi, http://tribune.com.pk/story/1194783/posters-calling-beheading-transwomen-surface-tariq-road/.

Nayab, D. 2011. "Estimating the Middle Class in Pakistan," Pakistan Institute of Development Economics, Working Paper 2011:77, Islamabad, http://pide.org.pk/pdf/Working%20Paper/WorkingPaper-77.pdf.

Pakistan Center for Philanthropy. 2012. "Individual Philanthropy in the Punjab," Islamabad.

Pakistan Center for Philanthropy. 2015. "Corporate Philanthropy in Pakistan: 15 Years, 2000–2014," Islamabad.

Rasheed, F. and A. F. Ali. 2013. *Khwaja Sira Socio-Economic Rehabilitation Program: Progress Report* (Lahore: Akhuwat).

Sen, A. K. 1977. "Rational Fools: A Critique of the Behavioral Foundations of Economic Theory," *Philosophy & Public Affairs*, 6(4), 317–344.

4 Critiques of conventional microcredit[1]

Introduction

This chapter reviews critiques of microcredit from various perspectives. Since we focus on critiques, we only briefly review some of the empirical studies supportive of microcredit. Our focus on critiques is both chronological and thematic. The key themes are the appropriation of microcredit by neo-liberalism in the 1980s as a mechanism to push back on the state centric basic human needs approach that had gained popularity as a heterodox development alternative in the 1970s.[2] To summarize, if the poor could be facilitated by microcredit to become market players to cater to their own needs, the state's role in the provision of basic needs becomes moot and the centrality of the market in development is secured.

While this was a win-win for neo-liberalism, there was yet another dividend to be gained from hence restructuring the focus of development policy for poverty alleviation. Western scholars, in partnerships with feminist scholars from the third world, had made great gains in the 1970s, and female empowerment had been put center stage as an outcome of gender and development scholarship.[3] Neo-liberalism appropriated the theme of female empowerment by asserting that it was intrinsically facilitated by microcredit.

The initial practitioners of microcredit found women were much better clients in terms of repayments and hence in reducing organizational transactions cost. Feminist scholars had empirically shown that the needs of the household were much better served when women had access to resources, and so there was a strong social justification for the focus of microcredit on women. Hence microcredit was a bonanza for neo-liberalism. It not only enabled a push back of state centric development but acquired a halo by associating itself via microcredit with poverty alleviation and female empowerment.

In terms of the chronology, we first explore the critical studies that expose how microcredit unwittingly became incorporated into the neo-liberal agenda. We say unwittingly because the original intent of microcredit was quite clearly poverty alleviation. But microcredit was unable to be self-financing due to the high transactions cost and hence organizational costs of reaching the rural poor in far-flung areas on the one hand and the self-evident ceiling that had to be imposed on lending rates charged on loans to the poor on the other hand. This opened the door to donors like the World Bank and its partner donor organizations, who had a different vision, to hijack the microcredit movement.

Yunus (2002, pp. 496–501), widely credited to be the modern founder of microcredit in the 1970s, sought to reject the view that entrepreneurship is a special trait and argued that the self-employed poor would be able to take care of themselves and enhance their assets and wealth if they had access to credit. Thus, the central premise in support for microcredit was that, in principle, all poor people could be entrepreneurs. But Yunus's concern was quite clearly with poverty alleviation, and this remained true even in 2015 when he advocated for the creation of a poverty museum once his vision was realized.[4]

Even so, Yunus and the microcredit movement were logical partners of neo-liberalism. His avidly pro-market and pro-entrepreneurial stance and his strong (in our view naïve) anti-welfare position made him, and other microcredit organizations that emulated the Grameen Bank microcredit model, willing partners of neo-liberalism.

However, the honeymoon period of this partnership did not last long since it was premised on providing subsidized funds to development NGOs for on-lending to the poor. Subsidies as market interventions and potential fiscal burdens are ideologically repugnant to neo-liberalism, and by the 1990s, when financialization was well underway, the World Bank followed the market-oriented logic of its economic philosophy and pushed for the sustainability of the organizations delivering microcredit and opening up microfinance delivery to for-profit enterprises.

In so doing, they shifted the focus from poverty alleviation or sustainable livelihoods to the financial sustainability of organizations delivering the microcredit. There was an implicit assumption that sustainable organizations, preferably operating as for-profit entities, delivering microcredit would also address poverty alleviation. This led to another push-back from critical scholars and financialization thus represents another theme of this review.

Microcredit had lost at least some of its sheen by the turn of the 21st century. Some scholars critiqued it for having lost sight of its earlier vision not only because they were forced to by the donors but because of intrinsic organizational motivations. Thus, upper management seemed more focused on its own agenda of empire building than with poverty alleviation. Another

Critiques of conventional microcredit

line of criticism was that microcredit was simply over-hyped and that it had intrinsic limitations as a development initiative and not really a success story. We explore these critiques as additional themes.

A review of the vast literature on microcredit suggests that Islamic instruments are being considered as an alternative in general terms and also in specific country contexts. Much of this literature on Islamic microfinance so far is prescriptive (what should be done?) rather than empirical. Akhuwat in this regard is now the largest organization attempting to provide an alternative to conventional microcredit and hence our focus on it.

To summarize, we first briefly review studies supportive of microcredit from various perspectives. Next, we turn to our objective, which is to critically evaluate microcredit chronologically and thematically. The themes are the appropriation of the microcredit movement by neo-liberalism and, by associating with it, becoming a champion of poverty alleviation and female empowerment. Since these critiques are often overlapping, we consider them jointly. The World Bank has pushed its pro-market agenda even further in the age of financialization and shifted the focus of attention to the sustainability of microcredit organizations and away from the beneficiaries of these organizations who thus became secondary and often collateral damage in this organizational restructuring.

We also explore the more recent criticisms that the original purpose of microcredit is being subsumed by organizational agendas and that microcredit has inherent limitations as a development initiative and not really a success story. We next briefly review Islamic microfinance in which Akhuwat looms large.

Islamic microfinance in general and Akhuwat in particular have claimed that they address the criticisms leveled at conventional microcredit. We draw on our critical review to summarize what these claims are and turn in the following chapters to describe the Akhuwat model and then to address these claims among other research questions explored.

Supportive studies

Several econometric studies concluded that micro-credit had a positive impact on women in general or on female empowerment in particular. Empowerment in these studies is generally defined instrumentally utilizing various outcome indicators such as mobility, network participation, resource control, decision making or bargaining power.[5] Notable among these studies that used instruments to control for selection bias are Ackerley (1995); Amin, Beker and Bayes (1998); Montgomery (2005); Pitt, Khandker and Cartwright (2006); Khan and Lutfan (2007); Li, Gan and Hu (2011); and Khandker and Samad (2014).

Swain and Wallentin (2009) defined empowerment as the ability of women to challenge social norms to improve their well-being. With innovative use of ordinal variables to identify empowerment, they estimated a structural model and concluded that participating in a Self Help Group[6] that provided microcredit enhanced empowerment over a three-year period compared to a non-participating control group.

Some authors found evidence indicating that credit to women had a positive impact on the well-being of children while this did not hold for credit to men. Guha-Khasnobis and Hazarika (2007) summarized such research, and their own findings and showed a positive correlation between credit to women and the long-term nutrition status of young girls but found no impact for credit to men. Armendáriz and Roome (2008, pp. 108–113) also reviewed studies that suggested more enhanced household and children's welfare from the expenditure of income controlled by women.

Various studies, supportive in principle, have focused on how microcredit could be made more effective. For example, Johnson (2005) suggested that in general a gendered approach to microcredit is required and, more specifically, emphasized that gendered analysis would identify different needs in different contexts such as skills training, market access, contract enforcement or child care facilities. Holvoet (2005) suggested that social group mediation is more likely to shift decision making from one that is norm guided to joint or female centered. Li, Gan and Hu (2011) identified threshold loan size as important to loan effectiveness.

Kabeer's (2001) definition of empowerment drew on the conceptualization of the human development indicators in that her concern was with the extension of the range of choices open to women and how microcredit contributed to that. This was consistent with her viewing empowerment not only as a process (managing loans) but also as an outcome. She also supported Sen's (1990) conflict–co-operative model of household decision making, and it is here that some of her findings from Bangladesh were novel.[7] For example, she found genuine solidarity within the household with women working to make men succeed as an investment in the household. Similarly, non-married women viewed an investment in household males as an insurance policy.

Aslanbeigui, Oakes and Uddin (2010) suggested that most concepts of empowerment used in the literature were fraught with logical inconsistencies, and using ten ethnographic case histories made a case that observing well-being and change should be based on intergenerational long-term observations. All the case histories in their small sample suggested that women with long histories of getting credit (16 to 23 years) expressed great satisfaction with the credit and were all much more prosperous than when they got their first loan.[8] While there are many more supportive empirical studies, we have only highlighted some of the main ones since the focus of this review is on the critiques of microcredit.

Critiques of microcredit[9]

The neo-liberal appropriation

Mayoux (1999), Iserlees (2003) and Johnson (2005) viewed the microcredit initiative to have been co-opted to push a neo-liberal agenda of paring down the state as explained above. Rankin (2001, p. 20) argued that microcredit transformed "beneficiaries with social rights" into "clients" responsible for themselves and their families. Three decades of feminist research showed that women contributed the bulk of production labor in agrarian societies, used their income to better effect for household well-being than men and were more likely to pay back loans. These findings she suggested were instrumentally used to justify microcredit for women by multilateral or bilateral donor organizations and their local NGO partners. Women's solidarity groups were similarly instrumentally used to reduce the transaction costs for the microcredit agencies rather than to raise consciousness of gender oppression and social change (Rankin, 2002, pp. 11–12).

Rankin and Shakya (2008) presented a nuanced analysis of how market-driven microfinance pushed by multilateral agencies and bilateral donors embodying neo-liberal ideology transformed development finance in rural Nepal. The original developmentalist conception of development finance, internalized by the economic bureaucracy, was one that viewed farmers as social citizens with rights to credit. Providing this credit was one mechanism the state could use for engaging in affirmative action, redistribution and providing social protection.

This progressive view was battered by the neo-liberal narrative of elite capture, clientalism, corruption, bureaucratic inefficiency, unsustainable subsidies and therefore the fiscal burden that state-owned development banks represented. The broader financial transformation entailed deregulation, opening banking to FDI (foreign direct investment) and a supportive legislative framework. Microfinance became the face of this financial transformation in rural areas.

Rankin and Shakya observed that although microcredit is inherently anti-statist, it depends on the state to succeed. Just as this observation applies more broadly to for example macroeconomic or trade policy, it also applies to the legislative, programmatic and regulatory reform needed for microfinance. They also pointed out that in the context of microfinance neo-liberalism does not spread as a "smooth, monolithic, or inevitable process" (p. 74). Its establishment requires the agency of the state, foreign and local partners in the periphery or L/MICs (low/middle income countries), and they documented how resistances and critiques could emerge in specific contexts. For example, in Nepal's case, progressive economic bureaucrats were resistant to the state withdrawing from its function in providing social protection. Charusheela and Danby (2006) argued that there are no hard and fast distinctions between women's productive and reproductive roles or between market and non-market activities, and a neo-liberal pushing back of state services in this context lessened the effectiveness of micro-credit outcomes as household resources were allocated to meet needs earlier provided by the state.

Goetz and Sen Gupta (1996) defined empowerment in terms of female ability to manage the loan they got. Based on this definition, they found that full or significant control was retained by only 37 percent. They found that control was mostly with men, but that the burden of repayment was borne by women. Because men were harder to locate and could turn violent when confronted, women were preferred as recipients but were not the true beneficiaries. However, since women were responsible for repayments, this resulted in household tension.

As women pressured the men for repayment, domestic violence against women was often the outcome. Furthermore, if women drew on domestic savings for repayment, this could be at the expense of expenditure on better nutrition, health and education for their children. The conclusion of this study was that instead of empowerment or a fundamental transformation in gender roles, men who already had access to women's labor now attained access to their capital also.

Even in situations where women did have entrepreneurial potential, limited mobility for cultural reasons meant that they did not have market access. The lack of such access limited what they could do with credit and perpetuated the dependence on men. The authors conceded that access to credit could raise women's leverage in the household and that could be parlayed into a coping and survival mechanism in cases of extreme poverty and dependence.

According to Montgomery, Bhattacharya and Hulme (1996), only 9 percent of first-time female borrowers were primary managers of loan-funded income generating activities. They also found that access to credit did little to change women's control over household finances. Rahman (1999) documented increased oppression of female clients of Grameen Bank in Bangladesh. Women were pressured by lending institutions to ensure timely payments. In a number of cases, such pressure led to "loan recycling" (borrowing from family or friends, other programs, or money lenders) to maintain timely payments and an increase in household indebtedness.

Parmer (2003) challenged the notion of empowerment as something that could be granted or externally induced. She argued that empowerment is internal and based on socially and personally overcoming oppression within the family and society. Since oppression is premised on class and gender relations, she suggested that change would require a broad social transformation in these relations via social mobilization.

More specifically, based on empirical research in Bangladesh, she found that microcredit was supposed to build group solidarity but actually created tensions resulting from peer group pressure, even to the extent of mutual interference in consumption patterns. In extreme cases, she found females detained in loan centers, shaming the women and the family.[10] This created tension within the household and women were at times subject to physical abuse. The centers, run by males, reinforced male hierarchies with the women required to call the loan officer "sir" and to submit to various demands even if they were proffered as self-improvement. She concluded that women were in fact doubly oppressed. They were oppressed first within the household by the males who pressured women to join the microcredit organizations and beat them if they did not qualify for larger loans. Second, they were oppressed by the microcredit organizations that passed monitoring costs on to women to keep their own monitoring and transactions costs low.

Garikipati (2008), using evidence from SHGs (self-help groups) in two drought-prone villages in India, pointed to an "impact paradox" evident in the empirical literature on gender and microcredit, i.e. that it reduced household vulnerability but did not necessarily enhance female empowerment. Her own empirical work confirmed this paradox. Exploring the mechanisms, she suggested that microcredit enhanced the gender asset ownership divide in favor of men and thus reduced female empowerment. Hence, a key policy recommendation emanating from her study was a focus on female asset ownership.

Additionally, beyond just being an ineffective tool and lacking relative context, Morduch (1999) argued that microcredit capitalized on women's lack of communal mobility compared to men because they were easier to trace for repayment purposes. Thus it is fundamentally promoted as a means for enabling empowerment on the surface, but instead institutionalized the problem of inequality more rather than grappling with its foundations and rethinking established normative structures.

Financialization

Financialization as a term became popular in depicting a changing economy since the 1980s such that financial capital subordinated industrial capital and the other real sectors of the economy in HICs (high-income countries). Along with this, it implies the push for capital mobility, financial liberalization and capital market broadening and deepening in emerging economies and the inter-linkages of the financial sectors of these economies with HICs financial sectors to facilitate a smooth flow of funds. This process reached a peak in 2007 in the United States with the housing crisis brought on partly by reckless financial engineering. Regulatory attempts were subsequently made in HICs to tame finance so that it did not pose a systemic risk to the real economy.

Financialization in the microcredit sector was twinned with another market oriented development fashion that caught on at the turn of the century. The catch phrase popularized by Prahalad (2004) entailed multinationals marketing "to the bottom of the pyramid." In the microcredit context, financialization implied welcoming for-profit delivery of microfinance and enabling metropolitan financial centers to have a stake in this booming business.

Rankin and Shakya (2008), using the Nepalese context, suggested that this neoliberal narrative struck a chord with progressive actors disillusioned with the state and they were co-opted in the rural microfinance movement as leaders of market-based financial NGOs who saw themselves as serving the poor by providing outreach but doing so in a sustainable way. The underlying assumption is that the poor can afford the interest rate necessary for the financial sustainability of the microfinance organizations, the primary neo-liberal objective.

Sinclair (2012) presented a personalized account, based on his experience of working in the sector, of initially having been enamored by microfinance and his subsequent dis-affection. The latter occurred because of the increasing commercialization of the sector as it became a US$70 billion industry. He viewed the microfinance movement to have been increasingly hijacked by profiteers in the 1990s. Bateman (2010, chapter 5) critiqued the new wave of commercial microfinance 'sans subsidy' that has been adopted by organizations like Grameen. He argued that this was rapidly replacing the older vintage of poverty oriented and subsidized NGO-led microfinance.[11]

These new wave financiers banked on the respectability provided by the UN, the Nobel Peace Prize received by Muhammad Yunus and the Grameen Bank, as the architects of the microfinance movement, and celebrities who joined the bandwagon. Many in the West put forward their funds by being informed that they were "doing well by doing good." In fact, the social enterprise funds were mobilized for exploiting the poor by charging interest rates up to 100 percent or more on "sub-sub-sub-prime" loans. Sinclair cited Muhammad Yunus (p. 11) as saying, "I never imagined that the microfinance sector would give rise to its own breed of loan sharks."[12] Saving accounts are a key instrument in this new wave of microfinance and the large differential between the borrowing and lending rate is the financial sustainability mechanism.

Roy (2010) depicted the merging of the Bangladesh model, where credit was perceived as a human right, to the World Bank initiated CGAP (Consultative Group to Assist the Poor) model in which financial sustainability of the organization became the focus. She documented (pp. 44–56; \Chapter 5) how securitization enabled large international NGOs like Grameen, BRAC and ASA to raise "poverty capital". Microcredit (now microfinance with saving accounts included) has become an asset class in global financial markets, delivering for social investment funds, that meet the double bottom line (i.e. "did well by doing good"). These international NGOs managed risk in this new "financialized" world where donor funding, subsidies and interest rate caps were eliminated.

Weber (2014, pp. 448–452) also explored the role played by CGAP as a standard setter in pushing financial liberalization as a commercial activity in LICs (low-income countries). She documented that the World Bank was aware of the intrinsic scale ineffectiveness of microcredit in creating employment but in Bangladesh supported it as a mechanism for the informal sector to absorb displaced workers in the structural adjustment led privatization drive. The plan was to both dampen the resistance to the privatization and at the same time convert grant driven microcredit into financially sustainable microfinance.

Nissanke (2002) reviewed the literature and identified a tension between the two goals donors pushed for microcredit, i.e. financial sustainability and poverty alleviation. Trying to attain the first inevitably meant compromising the second and hence increasingly the poorest got excluded from programs. Operationally, this tradeoff was manifested in the incentive structure the field staff was confronted with. Since financial sustainability was privileged, they had an incentive to avoid areas and individuals that might represent poor credit risk.

Marr (2002) pointed to, based on her research in rural Peru, the difficulty of gathering information in a peer group context. Severe sanctions were used to attain high repayment rates. This undermined group solidarity and in practice resulted in the exclusion of the poorest from groups. Serrano-Cinca et al (2013) confirmed the existence of the poverty penalty in microfinance, a concept that the poor generally pay more than the non-poor to access goods and services. Their empirical work was based in Colombia, and they found that even allowing for high administrative costs, high risk and the need to establish financial sustainability, the poverty penalty persisted. The authors attributed the poverty penalty to low efficiency and the profit motive of the MFIs.

Wichterich (2012) explored the for-profit microfinance sector in Andhra Pradesh (AP), India. The sector grew rapidly and at times piggy backed on the solidarity and community-based saving and loan organizations (bank-linked self-help groups). The for-profit organizations marketed the high recovery rates and charged interest rates as high as 40 percent and hence mobilized footloose funds seeking high returns after the 2007–2008 financial crash in the West.

Loans were pushed aggressively by several players in the market, and the ability to recycle debt sustained a high repayment rate for a while. Ironically, the lenders of last resort were village money lenders charging even higher interest rates of up to 50 percent. Eventually, crushed by indebtedness, some women committed suicide. Only a third of the loans were for income generation, and in any case market saturation (see below) reduced the chances of success.

Once the bubble burst and the sector expansion came to a grinding halt, politicians, who had done little to regulate the predation, attacked the financial companies. Ghosh (2013, p. 1214), in documenting the same crisis in Andhra Pradesh, India, pointed out that once regulations were put in place, the aggressive lending, loan recycling, and coercive collection methods were checked and interest capping introduced, the MFIs (microfinance institutions) became less viable.

Is microcredit a success story?

Bateman and Chang (2012) argued that microcredit is destructive rather than simply a benign but ineffectual development initiative. They suggested that it draws resources away from activities more likely to attain sustained economic growth based on the experience of countries that in the last century managed to attain catch up growth such as Japan and Korea. These include activities that entail economies of scale, forward and backward linkage, shift to higher value added activities and technological learning.

Instead, microcredit encourages informalization with attendant problems of a lack of regulations and a shrinking tax base. The fallacy of composition (what works for one does not necessarily work for all) ensured excess supply of commodities the loans were used for and hence low returns resulted in high indebtedness. Thus, an activity that might have worked for one or a few was rid of returns when more broadly engaged in locally.

Bateman (2010, p. 95) further argued that aggressively pushing microfinance also drew away funds from much more productive small- and medium-sized enterprises that could generate employment.[13] Chang (2010) elaborated further on this theme by arguing that palliatives like microcredit do not lead to authentic development that entails developing productive and technological capacity that diversifies the economy.

Karnani (2011, p. 81) indicated there is no evidence to support Yunus's premise of entrepreneurship being possible for all, and, given the bleak circumstances they live in, he argued that this makes even the natural entrepreneurs among the poor more risk averse. Much of the microcredit driven activity has low entry barriers, subject to low capital use, low productivity and intense competition. This barely ensures survival leave alone promoting a dynamism that creates additional assets, wealth and livelihoods as argued by Yunus.

The supportive studies cited in the first section above are impact assessments that concluded that microcredit delivered on its promises of improving household well-being and female empowerment. However, other econometric studies done equally carefully have disputed these findings. For example, Sharif (2004) showed that microcredit led to very limited "empowerment" (defined functionally). She concluded that norms change slowly and these programs can only have a limited impact in the short run. Banerjee et al. (2009) used randomized evaluation as an alternative way of controlling for selection and, based on a study of 104 slums (half randomly selected for the microcredit initiative) of Hyderabad, India, concluded that microcredit had no impact on women's decision making. Banerjee, Karlan and Zinman (2015) put together a special issue of the *American Economic Review, Journal of Applied Economics*, that contained six randomized evaluations, and the summary suggested a "lack of evidence of transformative effects on average borrowers" (p. 3).

Organizational agendas undermining poverty alleviation

Karim (2011) critiqued Bangladeshi "development" NGOs for serving their own agendas instead of the poor in whose name they raised funds.[14] She argued that these NGOs represented a shadow government or "quasi sovereign" actors in the rural economy who had distanced themselves from their original mission of poverty alleviation. Unlike true grassroots community organizations that empower the poor and women by working with and teaching them and building their confidence, these NGOs treated poor women as objects who served their own fund raising, diversification and corporate empire-building purposes. In keeping with this attitudinal change, there appeared to be a trend among these NGOs towards serving the middle class that represented a more reliable clientele for foreign multinationals pursuing profit at the "bottom of the pyramid."

Fernando (2006, p. 28) pointed out that in some Bangladeshi villages, NGOs delivering microcredit were referred to as "new *Zamindars* (land lords)" and "New East India Company" indicating that they were purely interested in squeezing the "'blood' from the poor." Flynn (2007) supported this critique and argued that commercial microcredit had become a part of what she referred to as neo-liberal "charity washing." In her view, for-profit global capital got direct access to the global poor using the cover of "financial inclusion" that microcredit provided.[15]

Another critical book by Faraizi, Rahman and McAllister (2011) is in the same vein. Based on two Bangladeshi village studies, they found the organizational staff to function in a disciplined manner as oppressive debt collectors but that essentially the microcredit project delivered for the organization rather than the subjects notwithstanding exceptions. Polished public relations and competent research departments created the knowledge that served the NGOs, while the latter served the purpose of extending the reach of capitalism within the existing exploitative social structure oppressive of women.

Karnani (2011) argued that both non-profit and commercial micro-credit organizations operate under monopolistic or oligopolistic market structures. This he argued accounted for the high interest rates rather than the high transactions cost due to the small loan size, lack of information and poor infrastructure. He cited evidence showing a high variation in costs holding loan size and location constant. In fact these organizations got away with an effective interest rate that was much higher than the stated rate due to a lack of competition, regulation, and low borrower literacy rates.

Practices that results in a high effective interest rate include the lack of grace period, upfront security fees (deducted from loan amount), forced saving deducted from installments (with saving rate much lower than borrowing rate), insurance premiums (deducted) and devious accounting practices (interested changed on original rather than declining balance). Taking these and other practices into account, the effective interest rate for a stated rate of 15 percent is often greater than a 100 percent and could be as high as 200 percent in some cases. It is therefore not surprising that in the non-profit group, a stated 10 percent on the microcredit loans earned a return on equity greater than 35 percent.

Another trend he reported on is the anecdotal evidence across the globe on very harsh methods used to recover tardy repayments. These included beatings by thugs hired by collection agencies.[16] In group loans, it is the "solidarity groups" that applied the pressure as indicated above. Karnani therefore suggested a need to regulate the industry, including monitoring collection methods, interest caps and transparency (announcing effective interest rates). While he did not rule out the use of self-monitoring, donor and civil society pressure, he suggested that for L/MICs government regulations are likely to be most effective. As civil society develops and institutions mature, they can complement but not displace government regulations.

Islamic microfinance

There are various country case studies on Islamic microfinance that cover South Andaman Islands, Australia, Bosnia and Herzegovina, Bangladesh,

Indonesia, Kosovo, Malaysia, Pakistan, Sudan, Syria, Yemen and various other Middle Eastern countries.[17] In some Islamic populations, microcredit faced resistance because interest is popularly associated with *riba* (a broader concept than interest; see Chapter 8), which is deemed forbidden by Islam (Khan, 1987). The authors have personally observed such objections during fieldwork in Pakistan, and Parto and Regmi (2009) report of similar objections in Afghanistan.

While the literature on Islamic banking dates back to the 1970s, the literature on Islamic microfinance is relatively recent (turn of the century) and still sparse (only 47 studies cited by EconLit in September 2017). Since most of the studies are prescriptive, to date there is not much to review. Masyita and Ahmed (2013) compared conventional microfinance with Islamic microfinance client responses in Indonesia and found that notwithstanding stated preference for Islamic finance, in practice clients were motivated by economic variables (interest rate, collateral, size of loan) and quality of service and in this regard Islamic microfinance lagged as did the growth of Islamic microfinance relative to conventional microfinance.

Jamal and Sheikh (2013) cite 21 possible instruments of Islamic finance with *Qarz-e-Hassn* as one among them. With the exception of *Qarz-e-Hassn*, which Akhuwat engages in, most of the others, except perhaps *mudarabah* and *musharika*, depending on how they are implemented, have been viewed by purists as legal casuistry. *Musharika* and *mudarabah* are forms of profit-sharing which are permitted because returns are not fixed like interest and are based on assuming risk (see Chapter 8 for a fuller discussion). However, estimating profits in the case of small informal sector micro-enterprises run by entrepreneurs with limited or no education and who therefore rarely maintain accounts would be a fool's errand.

Roy (2010, pp. 173–178) documented the enormously successful *al-qard al-hasan* (*Qarz-e-Hassn*, benevolent loan) program run by the Hezbollah in southern Lebanon and in the southern suburbs of Beirut. It is run on Islamic principles and possibly the largest microcredit program in the Middle East and much admired by the development NGO community. Membership is based on a "subscription fee," and this along with jewelry as collateral and weekly visits from "volunteer sisters" assures repayment. This program comes closest to the implementation of the Akhuwat model, particularly since the beneficiaries are not confined to a particular sect.[18]

Before turning to the Akhuwat model and its performance in the next chapters, we summarize here the critiques of microcredit that Akhuwat claims to address. Conventional microcredit is charged with pushing loans and encouraging clients to get on a debt treadmill since high interest rates make the burden of repayment high. It creates tensions within the household as women are pushed by men to take more loans. Men who use the loans and subsequently default put the burden of repayment on women. It creates tensions within the community due to loan inter-dependence associated with peer group lending. Thus, instead of social capital being built, it is systematically undermined given the way incentives are structured. Since peer groups in conventional microcredit are self-selected and since there is a high premium on avoiding default, the poorest viewed as poor loan risks are excluded. Finally, as explained above, conventional microcredit organizations are charged for losing sight of the original mission of poverty alleviation and instead start to engage in empire building. They are also viewed as undermining the state's responsibility to citizens and becoming neo-liberal stooges. How well Akhuwat manages to avoid these and other pitfalls of conventional microcredit is the subject for the rest of this book.

Conclusion

This chapter reviews the various critiques of microcredit. We pursue a chronological and thematic approach. In terms of the chronology, the microcredit movement became an ideal development partner for neo-liberalism. It was consistent with a market friendly or anti-statist message and purported to empower poor women. This hijacking of the movement went further in the drive to incorporate the movement in the neo-liberal led financialization such that the focus of attention shifted from sustainable livelihoods to the profitability of the organizations delivering microcredit.

In time, the sheen of microcredit as a development initiative wore off notwithstanding the Nobel Prize awarded to its acknowledged founder, Muhammed Yunus, and the Grameen Bank that he founded. Critics charged that the development NGOs delivering microcredit were more interested in pursuing their own empire building agendas than poverty alleviation. Others argued that it was a flawed development initiative due to the fallacy of composition and that it drew away funds from more tried and tested development strategies and in this regard was therefore even destructive.

It is worth musing why neo-liberalism has become so dominant even though heterodox scholars have so widely critiqued the negative social outcomes of neo-liberal prescriptions more broadly and specifically in the context of microfinance. There are many answers to this question in various contexts. The one relevant in particular to the spread of financialization is the ability of neo-liberal organizations like the World Bank and bilateral donors like the USAID to recruit and retain the loyalty of foot soldiers in the bureaucracies in L/MICs to implement their programs.

The enormous resource base of neo-liberal multi-lateral and bi-lateral organizations enables them to select and fund the training of promising young bureaucrats both in the periphery and in the West – within the training institutes housed in their own organizations or in like-minded centers in academia. Cognitive dissonance does the rest since careers at home and abroad are built on ideological purity and the contacts this yields. Such ideological brainwashing ensures the hegemony of neo-liberal doctrine. Neo-liberalism is likely to remain dominant until the social exclusion and inequality it yields result in social movements that bring about systematic changes in particular contexts and more broadly.

Another reason is that the neo-liberal critique of state-led development has resonance. For many in the bureaucracy and the broader public, the neo-liberal narrative of elite capture, clientelism, corruption, bureaucratic inefficiency, unsustainable subsidies and therefore the fiscal burden that state-owned development banks represented rang true. Yet, the critique conflates the implementing agency with the vision. In seeking to emasculate the state via deregulation, liberalization, and privatization, it also throws out the progressive vision of social protection and redistribution that the state embodies. In its place, it imposes a retrogressive alternative that serves the interest of global capital and further immiserizes the poor.

These critiques of conventional microfinance are scathing, and so it is not surprising that an interest free Islamic alternative practiced in Lebanon (*al-qard al-husan*) has been so well received. Akhuwat is based on the same principle of charitable giving and purports to avoid the negative effects of microcredit identified from various perspectives in this chapter. In the rest of this book, we first elaborate on the Akhuwat model of microcredit and turn next to an empirical evaluation of its claims to represent a benign alternative to conventional microcredit.

Notes

1 Microcredit and microfinance are sometimes used interchangeably. The former is the original financial instrument targeted to the poor, while the latter is a broader term that includes credit but could also include other financial instruments like saving accounts, insurance, pensions and remittance services for the same target group. Refer to Flynn (2007) for an account of these products. Refer to Microcredit Summit Campaign for statistics on the spread of microfinance.
2 This is also characterized as a "rights based" approach.
3 Refer to eds. Beneria, Berik and Floro (2016), in particular the historical overview (chapter 1).
4 www.youtube.com/watch?v=rWZTpX8GyIM.
5 Refer to Kulkarni (2011, pp. 11–14) for a discussion of various views on empowerment.
6 Development NGO initiated self-help groups are an Indian innovation and more akin to village or community (subset of village) organizations facilitated by development NGOs in other South and Southeast Asian countries than the microcredit peer groups innovated by the Grameen Bank exclusively for microcredit. They represent a single-sex (generally female) platform that development

Conceptual and institutional issues

NGOs and the government can interface with for facilitating poverty alleviation initiatives via collective action. Their regular savings accumulate to a pool of capital that can be used for microcredit loans or the SHG platform can be used by a public sector or NGO financial agency to provide microcredit using peer pressure as social collateral.

7 Refer to Ngo and Wahhaj (2012) for a theoretical exploration of household bargaining in the context of microcredit access.
8 Since the Grameen Bank identified all the interviewees, it is likely that they talked to the star performers.
9 For a book length critical evaluations of microfinance, refer to ed. Fernando (2006), Roy (2010), Karim (2011) and Faraizi, Rahman and McAllister (2011).
10 Refer also to Karim (2008, 2011) on the appropriation of "honor" and "shame" by microcredit institutions to reduce transactions costs.
11 Refer to eds. Drake and Rhyne (2002) for broadly supportive accounts of commercialization. Commercialization occurs when NGOs become business oriented or when commercial ventures enter the field.
12 Rosenberg, Gonzalez and Narain (2009) reviewed the evidence and argued that such predatory rates were the exception rather than the rule in commercial microfinance.
13 Refer to Bastiaensen et. al. (2013) who explored microfinance in Nicaragua and endorsed Bateman and Chang, but their findings suggested the need for caution when making generalizations.
14 The prominent ones include Grameen (claims to be a bank but one that represents a "social business"), BRAC (Building Resources Across Communities), ASA (Association for Social Advancement) and Proshika.
15 Refer also to Cull, Demirguc-Kunt and Murduch (2009).
16 Reddy (2014, p. 110) indicated that the coercive recovery practices included abusive language, criminal trespass, kidnappings, wrongful confinement, criminal intimidation and assaults on females.
17 Refer to Khaleequzzaman and Shirazi (2012). Karim et. al (2008) provide descriptive statistics for 14 Muslim countries.
18 Roy made no mention of the interest-free nature of these loans and therefore of the essence of how this model differs from conventional microcredit.

References

Ackerly, B. A. 1995. "Testing the Tools of Development: Credit Programs, Loan Involvement and Women's Empowerment," *IDS Bulletin*, 26(3), 56–68.
Amin, R., S. Becker and A. Bayes. 1998. "NGO-Promoted Microcredit Programs and Women's Empowerment in Rural Bangladesh: Quantitative and Qualitative Evidence," *Journal of Developing Areas*, 32(2), 221–236.
Armendáriz, B. and N. Roome. 2008. "Gender Empowerment in microfinance," in S. Sundaresan (ed.), *Microfinance* (Northampton, MA: Edward Elgar).
Aslanbeigui, N., G. Oakes and N. Uddin. 2010. "Assessing Microcredit in Bangladesh: A Critique of the Concept of Empowerment," *Review of Political Economy*, 22(2), 181–204.
Banerjee, A. et al. 2009. "The Miracle of Microfinance? Evidence from a Randomized Evaluation," www.microfinancegateway.org/gm/document-1.9.34827/The%20miracle%20of%20micronance.pdf.

Banerjee, Abhijit, Dean Karlan and Jonathan Zinman. 2015. "Six Randomized Evaluations of Microcredit: Introduction and Further Steps," *American Economic Review, Applied Economics* 7(1).
Bastiaensen, J. et al. 2013. "After the Nicaraguan Non-Payment Crisis: Alternatives to Microfinance Narcissism," *Development and Change*, 44(4), 861–885.
Bateman, M. 2010. *Why Doesn't Microfinance Work? Destructive Rise of Local Neoliberalism* (London: Zed Press).
Bateman, M. and H-J. Chang. 2012. "Microfinance and the Illusion of Development: From Hubris to Nemesis in Thirty Years," *World Economic Review*, 1(September 6), 13–36.
Beneria, L., G. Berik and M. S. Floro, eds. 2016. *Gender, Development and Globalization: Economics as If All People Mattered* (New York: Routledge), 2nd edition.
Chang, Ha-Joon. 2010. "Hamlet Without the Prince of Denmark: How Development Has Disappeared from Today's 'Development' Discourse," Chapter 2 in S. R. Khan and J. Christensen (eds.), *Towards New Developmentalism: Market as Means Rather Than Master* (New York: Routledge).
Charusheela, S. and C. Danby. 2006. "A Through-Time Framework for Producer Households," *Review of Political Economy*, 18(1), 29–48.
Cull, R., A. Demirguc-Kunt and J. Morduch. 2009. "Microfinance Meets the Market," in T. A. Watkins and K. Hicks (eds.), *Moving Beyond Storytelling: Emerging Research in Microfinance* (Bingley, UK: Emerald).
Drake, D. and E. Rhyne, eds. 2002. *The Commercialization of Microfinance: Balancing Business and Development* (Bloomfield, CT: Kumarian Press).
Faraizi, A., T. Rahman and J. McAllister. 2011. *Microcredit and Women's Empowerment: Case Study of Bangladesh* (London: Routledge).
Fernando, J. L., ed. 2006. *Microfinance: Perils and Prospects* (New York: Routledge).
Flynn, P. 2007. "Microfinance: The Newest Financial Technology of the Washington Consensus," *Challenge*, 50(2), 110–121.
Garikipati, S. 2008. "The Impact of Lending to Women in Household Vulnerability and Women's Empowerment Evidence from India," *World Development*, 31(12), 2620–2642.
Ghosh, J. 2013. "Microfinance and the Challenge of Financial Inclusion for Development," *Cambridge Journal of Economics*, 37(6), 1203–1219.
Goetz, A. and R. Sen Gupta. 1996. "Who Takes the Credit?" Gender, Power, and Control Over Loan Use in Rural Credit Programs in Bangladesh," *World Development*, 24(1), 45–63.
Holvoet, N. 2005. "The Impact of Microfinance on Decision-Making Agency: Evidence from South India," *Development and Change*, 36(1), 75–102.
Iserlees, R. G. 2003. "Microcredit: The Rhetoric of Empowerment, The Reality of 'Development as Usual'," *Women Studies Quarterly*, 31(3/4), 38–57.
Jamal, A. A. N. and M. A. A. Sheikh. 2013. "Challenges Faced by the Model of Islamic Microfinance for the Development of Micro Entrepreneurs and SMEs in Rural Pakistan," *International SAMANM Journal of Finance and Accounting*, 1(3), 17–38.
Johnson, S. 2005. "Gender Relations, Empowerment and Microcredit: Moving on from a Lost Decade," *European Journal of Development Research*, 17(2), 224–248.

54 Conceptual and institutional issues

Kabeer, N. 2001. "Conflicts Over Credit: Re-Evaluating the Empowerment Potential of Loans to Women in Rural Bangladesh," *World Development*, 29(1), 63–84.

Karim, L. 2008. "Demystifying Microcredit: The Grameen Bank, NGOs, and Neoliberalism in Bangladesh," *Cultural Dynamics*, 20(5).

Karim, L. 2011. *Microfinance and Its Discontents: Women in Debt in Bangladesh* (Minneapolis: University of Minnesota Press).

Karim, N., M. Tarazi and X. Reille. 2008. "Islamic Microfinance: An Emerging Market Niche," The Consultative Group to Assist the Poor, Focus Note, Washington, DC.

Karnani, A. 2009. "Romanticizing the Poor Harms the Poor," *Journal of International Development*, 21(1), 76–86.

Karnani, A. 2011. "Microfinance Needs Regulation," *Stanford Social Innovation Review*, (Winter 2011), 48–53.

Khaleequzzaman, M. and S. N. Shirazi. 2012. "Islamic Microfinance – An Inclusive Approach with Special Reference to Poverty Eradication in Pakistan," *International Journal of Economics, Management and Accounting*, 20(1), 19–49.

Khan, O. and N. Lutfun. 2007. "A Breakthrough in Women's Bargaining Power: The Impact of Microcredit," *Journal of International Development*, 19(5), 695–716.

Khan, S. R. 1987. *Profit and Loss Sharing: An Economic Analysis of an Islamic Financial System* (Karachi: Oxford University Press).

Khandker, Shahidur R. and Hussain A. Samad. 2014. "Dynamic Effects of Microcredit in Bangladesh," Policy Research Working Paper, no. WPS 6821. Washington, DC: World Bank Group, http://documents.worldbank.org/curated/en/2014/03/19304457/dynamic-effects-microcredit-bangladesh.

Kulkarni, V. S. 2011, "Women's empowerment and microfinance: An Asian perspective study," Occasional Papers, Knowledge for Development Effectiveness, No. 13, Asia and Pacific Division, IFAD, Rome.

Li, X., C. Gan and B. Hu. 2011. "The Impact of Microcredit on Women's Empowerment in China," *Journal of Chinese Economic and Business Studies*, 9(3), 239–261.

Marr, A. 2002. "Microfinance and Poverty Reduction: The Problematic Experience of Communal Banking in Peru, SOAS Economics Research Working Papers," www.soas.ac.uk/economics/research/workingpapers/file28856.pdf.

Masyita, D. and H. Ahmed. 2013. "Why Is Growth of Islamic Microfinance Lower Than Its Conventional Counterparts in Indonesia?" *Islamic Economic Studies*, 21(1), 35–62.

Mayoux, L. 1999. "Questioning Virtuous Spirals: Micro-Finance and Women's Empowerment in Africa," *Journal of International Development*, 11(7), 957–984.

Montgomery, H. 2005. "Meeting the Double Bottom Line – The Impact of Khushhali Bank's Microfinance Program in Pakistan," Asian Development Bank Institute Policy Paper No. 8.

Montgomery, R., D. Bhattacharya and D. Hulme, 1996. "Credit For the Poor in Bangladesh: The BRAC Rural Development and Employment Program," in D. Hulme and P. Mosley (eds.), *Finance Against Poverty*, Vol. 2 (New York: Routledge).

Morduch, J. 1999. "The Microfinance Promise," *Journal of Economic Literature*, 37(4), 1569–1614.

Ngo, T. M. and Z. Wahhaj. 2012. "Microfinance and Gender Empowerment," *Journal of Development Economics*, 99(1), 1–12.

Nissanke, M. 2002. "World Institute for Development Economic Research (UNU-WIDER)," Working Papers: UNU-WIDE Research Paper DP2002/127, Helsinki, www.wider.unu.edu/stc/repec/pdfs/rp2002/dp2002-127.pdf.

Parmar, A. 2003. "Micro-Credit, Empowerment, and Agency: Re-Evaluating the Discourse," *Canadian Journal of Development Studies*, 24(3), 461–476.

Parto, S. and A. Regmi. 2009. "Microcredit and Reconstruction in Afghanistan: An Institutionalist Critique of Imported Development," in T. Natarajan, E. Wolfram and S. T. Fullwiler (eds.), *Institutional Analysis and Praxis: The Social Fabric Matrix Approach* (New York and London: Springer).

Pitt, M., S. R. Khandker and J. Cartwright. 2006. "Empowering Women with Micro Finance: Evidence from Bangladesh," *Economic Development and Cultural Change*, 54(4), 791–831.

Prahalad, C. K. 2004. *Fortune at the Bottom of the Pyramid: Eradicating Poverty Through Profits* (Upper Saddle River, NJ: Prentice Hall).

Rahman, A. 1999. "Micro-Credit Initiatives for Equitable and Sustainable Development: Who Pays," *World Development*, 27(1), 67–82.

Rankin, K. N. 2001. "Governing Development: Neoliberalism, Microcredit, and Rational Economic Woman," *Economy and Society*, 30(1), 8–37.

Rankin, K. N. 2002. "Social Capital, Microfinance, and the Politics of Development," *Feminist Economics*, 8(1), 1–24.

Rankin, K. N. and Y. B. Shakya. 2008. "Neoliberalizing the Grassroots? Microfinance and the Politics of Development in Nepal," in K. England and K. Ward (eds.), *Neoliberalization: States, Networks, Peoples* (Oxford: Wiley-Blackwell), pp. 48–76.

Reddy, N. 2015. "The Political Economy of Microfinance and Marginalized Groups: Implications of Alternative Institutional Strategies," in B. Harris-White and J. Heyer (eds.), *Indian Capitalism in Development* (New York: Routledge).

Rosenberg, R., A. Gonzalez and S. Narian. 2009. "The New Moneylenders: Are the Poor Being Exploited by High Microcredit Interest Rates?" in T. A. Watkins and K. Hicks (eds.), *Moving Beyond Storytelling: Emerging Research in Microfinance*. Contemporary Studies in Economic and Financial Analysis Volume 92 (Bingley: Emerald Group).

Roy, A. 2010. *Poverty Capital: Microfinance and the Making of Development* (New York: Routledge).

Sen, A. K. 1990. "Gender and Co-operative Conflicts," in I. Tinker (ed.), *Persistent Inequalities: Women and World Development* (Oxford: Oxford University Press).

Serrano-Cinca, C. et al. 2013. "Poverty Penalty and microfinance," Universite Libre de Bruxelles, Working Papers CEB: 13–029.

Sharif, N. R. 2004. "Microcredit Programs and Women's Decision Making Status: Further Evidence from Bangladesh," *Canadian Journal of Development Studies*, 25(3), 465–480.

Sinclair, H. 2012. *Confessions of a Microfinance Heritic: How Microlending Lost Its Way and Betrayed the Poor* (San Francisco: Beretta-Koehler Publishers, Inc.).
Swain, R. B. and F. Y. Wallentin. 2009. "Does Microfinance Empower Women? Evidence from Self Help Groups in India," *International Review of Applied Economics*, 23(5), 541–556.
Weber, H. 2014. "Global Politics of Microfinancing Poverty in Asia: The Case of Bangladesh Unpacked," *Asian Studies Review*, 38(4), 544–563.
Wichterich, C. 2012. "The Other Financial Crisis: Growth and Crash of the Microfinancial Sector in India," *Development*, 55(3), 406–412.
Yunus, M. 2002. "Poverty Alleviation: Is Economics Any Help? Lessons from the Grameen Bank Experience," in P. Athukorala (ed.), *The Economic Development of South Asia* (Northampton, MA: Edward Elgar), pp. 487–505.

5 The Akhuwat interest-free microcredit model

Introduction

Our focus in this chapter is to set out the Akhuwat model as a contrast to the standard microcredit model reviewed in Chapter 4. We explore in the next two chapters the ability of this model to evolve to respond to issues that arise at the grassroots level. We avoid extensively reviewing ground already covered elsewhere. For details on history, organizational structure, loaning methodology, operations and financial management, refer to the many documents on Akhuwat's website (www.akhuwat.org.pk), Akhuwat (2007) and to Zaidi et al. (2007, chapter 5, pp. 1–13).

As of August 2017, Akhuwat had provided loans to 2.1 million households (www.akhuwat.org.pk/progress_report.asp) and dispersed Rs. 45 billion (about $427 million at the September 12, 2017, exchange rate) in interest-free loans. Estimates suggest an average household size of 6.8,[1] so it has reached about 14 million people or approximately 7.5 percent of Pakistan's 2016 population of 198 million.

Another indicator of the scope of its operations is that by 2015 it had the third-largest number of active borrowers among listed microcredit organizations.[2] While the growth of microcredit in Pakistan has been very rapid from a small base, that of Akhuwat has been meteoric. Akhuwat started in 2001 and by July 2017 was serving 2.1 million borrowers as indicated above.

We start with an overview of the organization's mission and vision. We follow that with an overview of Akhuwat's success in numbers. We briefly turn to Akhuwat's organizational structure and how it operates and then review Akhuwat's interest free microcredit model as an alternative to conventional microcredit.

Mission and vision

Akhuwat was founded in 2001 and in 2003 opened its first branch in Township, Lahore (Harper et al., 2008). Its mission as stated on its website is "to alleviate poverty by empowering socially and economically marginalized families through interest free microfinance and by harnessing entrepreneurial potential, capacity building and social guidance." Its co-founder and Executive Director, Dr. Amjad Saqib, was seconded as a civil servant to a prominent government sponsored rural development non-governmental organization. During fieldwork, he encountered an elderly woman who insisted that she be granted an interest-free loan consistent with her religion and faith. Dr. Saqib and some friends fronted the loan from their own funds and her successful and inspirational use of the funds and timely repayment gave birth to the vision of the organization.

Its guiding principles encapsulate the vision of the organization as outlined by Dr. Amjad Sadiq in his book (2014, p. 32). The first principle is to provide interest free microcredit (*Qarz-e-Hassn*) to enable the economically poor to acquire a self-sustaining livelihood. It also plans in the future to provide the skills and support they need to actualize their full potential and abilities. Second, it uses underutilized local mosque/church infrastructure as centers for loan disbursement and as avenues for community participation. Third, the organization is infused across the board with a spirit of volunteerism which includes the service of the Board of Directors, Executive Director and founder and Steering Committees, field staff overtime, and professional and student volunteers. Fourth, it encourages its borrowers to donate to Akhuwat and so help their communities, once the borrowers themselves have gained enough economic prosperity and stability. However, these donations are neither compulsory nor meant to have any bearing on the borrower's credit profile. Finally, its programs are open to all irrespective or creed, caste or gender.

To these one could add a fifth, which is that of promoting inter-faith harmony. Members of its senior and junior staff are Christians, and accordingly Christmas celebrations are organized for Christian staff. This active inter-faith component of the organization via cross-faith hiring and merit-based promotions is rare in Pakistan. Dr. Saqib also draws on inter-faith parables to inspire his staff members. As narrated by one unit manager during our fieldwork, Dr. Saqib's message is that they "should turn the other cheek" in behavior to others or risk undermining the organization.

Akhuwat's success in numbers

Appendices 5.1–5.3 provide details of its progress to date in numbers. As indicated earlier, it has grown rapidly since its inception. Its total loan portfolio in nominal terms reached Rs. 45 billion by October 2017.[3] Similarly, borrowers and branches increased to 2.04 million and 674 respectively (Appendix 5.1). Donations in nominal terms increased from Rs. 1.5 million at inception to Rs 858.4 million in 2016–2017 (Appendix 5.3). It has maintained recovery rates of close to 100 percent, exceptionally high even for a microcredit organization (Appendix 5.2). It reports an operational cost of less than 10 percent, which compares well with an estimate of about double that for conventional microfinance institutions.[4]

Organization[5]

Structure

Akhuwat has 17 members of the Board of Directors that meet quarterly. The board is responsible for formulating and approving policy and providing guidance and direction on organizational issues. An Executive Committee consisting of three members meets every month for reviewing all administrative and operational issues of the organization. Three top executives– Chief Financial Officer (CFO), Chief Operating Officer (COO) and Chief Credit Officer (CCO) – play the central administrative role with 263 head office staff working under them.[6] As of September 2017, the CCO was supervising 20 regional managers, with 695 branch and 2,558 unit managers working under them.[7] Some branches have a steering committee comprised of eight to ten prominent individuals living in that area and two representatives from Akhuwat, generally the Area and the Branch Managers.

The Steering Committees are constituted to oversee branches and do so in a voluntary capacity. They may be important donors and hence stakeholders in the organization. Typically, the numbers of prominent citizens (often members of the Chambers of Commerce) on the committee far exceed the active members. The active members monitor, including with fieldwork and regular meetings with staff who provide written reports, to ensure policy implementation. They also engage in fund raising, make recommendation for recruitment of staff members and can make policy recommendations. They may make recommendations for loans, but acceptance of loan requests is entirely at the discretion of the field office using its regular procedures. If they recommend expansion to other areas where Akhuwat is not present, it is again based on standard methodology.

The organization believes that staff members are remunerated at market rates with a generous benefits package (see Chapter 8 for more on this). These benefits include medical and life insurance, a provident fund, access to credit including for motor cycles, and fuel expenses for official work. As of mid-2016, the staff size of this rapidly growing organization was 3,300.

Operations

Public awareness of the program is predominantly by word of mouth and announcements in local mosques and churches. The loan process for

60 Conceptual and institutional issues

business loans start with an application which is first evaluated by the unit manager based on whether the person is below the poverty line (as per the organization's internal poverty profiling, Appendix 6.1), has reliable social networks, is not involved in any illegal business and possesses requisite entrepreneurial abilities. The business plan is then evaluated, and the applicant's family is also interviewed to make sure that they know about the loan and support the business idea so that everyone who has potential to be affected by the loan in the household is aware of it from the on-set.

If the application is approved by the unit manager, it is forwarded to the branch manager who engages in a technical appraisal and then refers the application to the Loan Approval Committee comprising of the unit, branch and area mangers. The whole process takes almost three weeks to a month. Approval requires the applicant providing two guarantors from the local community or finding at least two members in the immediate neighborhood also wanting a loan, one of them being a home owner as an anchor for traceability in case the others move away. The disbursement for group loans is within two to three months in a mass function in a mosque or a church. For individual loans, a default option for those not able to be included in a group, the guarantors accompany applicants. The presence of the local community members, guarantors, mosque imams or church fathers provides moral pressure for loan repayment.

Up to 100–150 loans are collectively disbursed, and the function provides the organization the opportunity to provide guidance on social issues such as female education, social commitment, ethics, and environmental awareness. Repayment dates for installments can vary by branch, but for several we visited the due date was the seventh of each month. If the individual or group (collective) installment is not received, the unit manager contacts the loan recipient; and if the installment is still not received by the 10th, the social guarantor or group members are contacted.

Akhuwat used to charge a 5 percent service fee but abolished this in 2009 and currently charges only a fixed Rs. 100 non-refundable registration fee. There is a voluntary 1 percent contribution to a mutual support or *shirakat* fund (which most loan recipients contribute to, but the fee can be waived for those receiving small loans). In case of death, the loan is written off, funeral expenses covered and a stipend of Rs. 5,000 provided to the family. In case an accident results in a handicap, a wheelchair is provided when needed.

The standard loan (Rs. 10,000–50,000) is granted to the family (co-signed) for business ventures. As indicated in Appendix 5.4, the standard loan represents 97 percent of total loans. One percent of the loans are called liberation loans (up to Rs. 50,000), and these are designed to enable individuals to escape debt bondage from loan sharks. The remaining 2 percent are for essential housing renovation (Rs. 30,000–70,000), health or other emergency (quickly processed for expenses between Rs. 5,000–10,000), education (up to Rs. 25,000) or marriage expenses (up to Rs. 20,000). A silver loan of Rs. 50,000 is granted to successful borrowers in good standing to expand an enterprise.

Akhuwat manages to keep down operating costs by hiring field staff from nearby communities at market rates. The COO suggested in an interview that up to 20 percent of time spent working for the organization by the field staff is on a voluntary basis. Religious infrastructure (mosques or churches) are used for meetings, and so only small offices need to be maintained adjacent to these religious buildings. Furniture is very sparse, and floor seating is used. Top management works on a voluntary basis, and at the lower end student volunteers are welcomed and widely utilized. Containing overhead costs is especially important since Akhuwat has for the most part not solicited funds from foreign donors (see Chapter 8).

Akhuwat has been expanding rapidly based on community solicitations (see Appendix 5.1).[8] However, there is also replication by clones with the same social vision. Thus, Akhuwat is always on the look-out for local partners and like-minded people to start a branch in their own cities. In case a partner organization is found, Akhuwat provides training to the local staff and helps in setting up the branch. While leaving the operations to the partner organization, Akhuwat provides regular training and monitoring. Examples of organizations that have been inspired by Akhuwat are listed in Appendix 5.5.

The Akhuwat model as an alternative

Akhuwat was founded in Pakistan in 2001 to be consistent with Islamic ethical principles, but it also claims to address some of microcredit's other shortcomings discussed in Chapter 4.[9] As indicated in Chapter 1, Akhuwat draws contributions from *infaq* (voluntary giving) and in turn gives interest free *Qarz-e-Hassn* (literally beautiful loans), hence addressing Muslim objections to *riba* including interest. Charity underlies both the financial sustainability of the organization and its operational principle of interest-free loans.

Akhuwat also applies limited pressure for repayment (see Chapter 6). If households are found in dire straits, the loan is forgiven. While group loans do tap social capital like other microcredit organizations such as the Grameen Bank, it principally relies on imparting to its borrowers the Islamic ethic of responsibility to the community as encompassing worship. Worship involves God consciousness, but this is intended to induce right action (based on social solidarity and empathy) that in this case includes charitable giving and repaying loans. The "borrowers to donors" principle has been instituted to this end. Thus, instead of paying fixed interest, beneficiaries are encouraged to donate back in order to assist someone else like them.[10] Imparting these ethical principles prior to handing out the loans appears to be effective and repayment rates are reported to be higher than conventional microcredit (see Appendix 5.2).

Akhuwat has tapped into this context specific value system to build a revolving fund and uses this to provide small loans for enterprises in keeping with Islamic economic philosophy. The return of the loans then re-charges the revolving fund which also continues to grow as knowledge of the good work spreads and the broader community makes donations. As explained in our review of Akhuwat's accounts in Chapter 8, of late its credit pool has grown enormously with contributions from the government and a very modest contribution by comparison from an international charitable NGO.

We explain in Chapter 8 that the nature of the public-NGO partnership that Akhuwat has contracted enables it to charge a service fee on funds disbursed. In principle this should give it an incentive to disburse at a much higher rate and scale up. Nonetheless, our field investigation shows that it has continued to maintain the extremely conservative approach that it started out with when its credit pool was based entirely on private donations and it was free of any incentive to expand. It continues to exercise due diligence in selecting borrowers capable of establishing an owner operated enterprise. More revenue associated with more indebtedness would violate its underlying philosophy. In this regard the organization accepts its limitations of not being able to provide an unconditional right to assistance for all who seek it.

Many earlier borrowers become donors when their enterprise succeeded, and the ethic is to graduate from borrowing to donating, when possible, rather than to continue borrowing. Once again, the idea is not to keep borrowers continually engaged by incentivizing more and larger borrowing based on past repayments. Instead, success is premised on enabling borrowers to become independent and not need more loans from the organization. Nevertheless many respondents we talked to took multiple loans and intended to take future loans as well (Chapter 6).

Akhuwat also claims that since their loan is to the household rather than an individual, the responsibility within the household is shared. The loan therefore does not pit household members against each other but emphasizes their unity and common purpose and for the household to work collectively to enhance their own prosperity and meet their community responsibility (see Chapter 6).

Even though microcredit is a family undertaking, Akhuwat claims the principles of altruism and volunteerism are infused in the execution. Borrowers remind other community members of repayment dates, introduce new borrowers to the program, and assist loan officers in explaining the program to potential borrowers. It claims that via 'internships,' new borrowers are taught book-keeping, business location (for stores/carts), skills (embroidery/ stitching) and customer management. Borrowers have also pooled resources for food distribution, although we saw no evidence of this in our limited fieldwork.

The Akhuwat model of loan delivery encompasses another institutional innovation. Once applications for the loans are reviewed, those who qualify are invited to the community mosque, both men and women. This entails returning the mosque to its original purpose of being a community center but also keeps down transactions cost. To mark the simplicity of its ethical philosophy and to emphasize the lack of hierarchy, the lender and borrowers sit on the floor in an organic setting that facilitates solidarity between the staff and beneficiaries, instead of impersonal exchange. The tight-knit social fabric that is characteristic of these communities is thus preserved, instead of disrupted by the injection of finance and market principles.

The ceremony is not only held at mosques; disbursements are also often conducted at churches and shrines depending on the composition of the borrowing community.

After narrating the values of the organization and emphasizing community responsibility the checks are handed out by the loan officers or unit managers serving the particular community from which the loan applications were received. The loan officers engage on a personal level with the beneficiaries, serving a community of about 300, and are perceived as friends and advisors rather than as agents of a loan organization. This is an important work ethic instilled and emphasized by Akhuwat's human resource and training procedures for its staff. Staff is rotated and do not serve the community they hail from to prevent conflict of interest.

Upper management draws on volunteers that serve on an "honorary" basis (Munir, 2012). The organizational culture is infused with the principles of simplicity, egality, solidarity and community that it purports are central to its purpose and functioning. Thus, Sen's conceptual notion of commitment identified in Chapter 2 is embodied as an important operational feature.

By adopting a community-oriented approach, Akhuwat intends to be a source of support for its borrowers. Instead of repayment harassment as many microcredit firms have been accused of, it aims to foster mutual support and self-governance. As indicated above, the organization motivates borrowers to pay back their loans not out of fear of the consequences of harassment but rather by trying to make them realize their self-worth and self confidence in their own capacities to engage as involved citizenry of their communities. The organization realizes the operational importance of encouraging the borrower to employ the loan for its intended purpose and understand that by doing so, and subscribing to the Akhuwat loan methodology, the borrowers are not only serving their own interests but benefit their communities.

Sermons prior to loan disbursements in religious centers are an important mechanism for this. Akhuwat aims to cultivate a spirit which promotes consciousness in its borrowers by encouraging them to uplift themselves by uplifting their community vis-a-vis timely repayment and donating back to the organization, hence moving beyond competition and enterprise. By adopting this approach, in principle it addresses an important critique of conventional microcredit of eroding community solidarity (see Chapter 4 for critique and Chapter 6 for the operational evaluation of this approach using survey data).

Akhuwat claims that it is not concerned with empire building and encourages replication by training and mentoring other civil society organizations interested in its approach. According to the CCO, replications opt for a name of their choosing. As earlier indicated Akhuwat provides training, shares its manuals, helps with monitoring, auditing and financial literacy. As of the summer of 2015, more than 20 organizations had replicated the Akhuwat model (Appendix 5.5). The Islah Foundation had opened 15 branches and adopted Akhuwat-Islah Foundation as its name. According to the CCO, "Some have even extended the model and are doing better work than us. For instance Zaadira gives breakfast at disbursements and does not charge any application fee."

The funds collected based on public, borrower and staff contributions are donated to Akhuwat's credit pool. As Akhuwat's reputation spread by word of mouth, there has been an impressive growth in donations to Akhuwat Financial Services. In nominal terms, these went up 572-fold from 2001–2002 to their peak in 2016–2017 (from Rs. 1.5 million to Rs. 858 million; see Appendix 5.3).

Summary

Akhuwat has developed a unique model of microcredit based on the preceptoral mechanism of moral guidance for staff and borrowers identified in Chapter 2. This has several inherent advantages. It can keep transactions costs and overheads down and repayment rates high. It has an ambitious goal of turning borrowers into donors and hence enhances its credit pool or revolving fund. The amounts involved, as documented in Chapter 8, are so far very modest but nonetheless of symbolic importance. Further, by inculcating moral guidance of compassion and volunteerism, it hopes to create mutually supportive communities.

Akhuwat does not assume that all individuals have the gift of entrepreneurship unlike other microcredit organizations. Of the various proposals it receives, it carefully vets and selects only those that it anticipates have a chance of succeeding. In so doing, it anticipates that the entrepreneur might contribute to the uplift of the community by creating livelihoods.

Appendices 5.1–5.3 and 5.5 paint a picture of remarkable success for a young organization. The numbers are all off the charts. Its portfolio, borrowers and branches have shown an impressive pace of success since its inception. It continues to maintain very high repayment rates, and within-country donor contributions to its credit pool have also shown a stratospheric rise. Insofar as emulation is a marker of success, there have been a large number of spontaneous replications, which it has welcomed and assisted rather than viewed as a threat.

However, it is important to go beyond the numbers. In the next two chapters, we breathe life into these numbers by using qualitative and quantitative information gathered in the field and in so doing evaluate Akhuwat's success using several other criteria as well.

Appendix 5.1

Expansion since inception

Year	Loan portfolio	Borrowers	Branches
2001–02	1,895,000	192	1
2002–03	2,791,300	282	2
2003–04	8,504,000	832	4
2004–05	31,811,000	3,124	7
2005–06	66,020,700	6,264	11
2006–07	89,935,600	8,674	18
2007–08	122,445,242	11,388	20
2008–09	164,226,000	13,821	22
2009–10	251,808,800	21,073	36
2010–11	418,211,100	34,194	77
2011–12	1,137,684,000	67,683	153
2012–13	2,580,467,000	159,138	254
2013–14	4,047,109,100	234,883	289
2014–15	7,310,527,000	367,798	356
2015–16	11,205,522,500	496,458	499
2016–17	43,727,601,142	2,039,681	674

Source: Akhuwat head office

Appendix 5.2

Akhuwat recovery rates since inception (%)

Year	Rate
2001–02	100.00
2002–03	99.95
2003–04	99.90
2004–05	99.95
2005–06	99.90
2006–07	99.50
2007–08	99.37
2008–09	99.50
2009–10	99.85
2010–11	99.85
2011–12	99.86
2012–13	99.87
2013–14	99.85
2014–15	99.93
2015–16	99.93
2016–17	99.94

Source: Akhuwat head office

Appendix 5.3

Donated funds since inception (million Rs., current)

Year	Amount
2001–02	1.50
2002–03	1.80
2003–04	7.10
2004–05	10.90
2005–06	28.30
2006–07	17.72
2007–08	23.98
2008–09	36.17
2009–10	53.00
2010–11	108.37
2011–12	97.71
2012–13	85.04
2013–14	103.00
2014–15	148.60
2015–16	352.47
2016–17	858.43

Source: Akhuwat head office

Notes: The Chief Financial Officer speculated that the drop after 2010–2011 might have resulted from bidding for and winning big competitive government grants. This focused management attention towards managing the funds and away from private fund raising for a while.

Appendix 5.4

Percentage distribution of loan products

Purpose of Loan	Percentage
Enterprise Loan	97.38
Education Loan	0.31
Emergency Loan	0.00
Health Loan	0.24
Liberation Loan	0.97
Marriage Loan	0.74
School Loan	0.35
Total	100

Source: Akhuwat head office

Appendix 5.5
Akhuwat replications

List of Akhuwat Replications
Kawish Welfare Trust
Al Nur Umar Welfare Trust
Sojhro
ECI Pakistan
Heral Buniyaad
Decent Welfare, Gujrat
Naimat Foundation
Akhuwat Karachi
Brooke International, Pakistan
Muslim Aid, Pakistan
Rural Development Organization, Dera Ghazi Khan
Din Group

Source: Helping Hands, Akhuwat head office

Notes

1 "Pakistan Microfinance Review 2015," www.arcgis.com/home/item.html?id=8aead66ab8894fa49dbf3f92e1adbfc3.
2 Pakistan Average Household Size, http://microfinanceconnect.info/assets/articles/a7248cfa411a34074d03aafd4ed7cd6c.pdf, exhibit 2.3, p. 22.
3 We inquired about the big jump between 2016 and 2017 across the board, and the Chief Credit Officer assured us that there was no mistake. He said that the rise in the numbers can be explained by "Akhuwat's expanding by every passing day due to some new projects, new branches, system's efficiency & better funds management."
4 The median OER of MFIs reporting to MIX (Microfinance Information Exchange) Market for 2006 was about 19 percent (www.cgap.org/sites/default/files/CGAP-Technical-Guide-Measuring-Results-of-Microfinance-Institutions-Minimum-Indicators-That-Donors-and-Investors-Should-Track-Jul-2009.pdf, p. 11 [downloaded November 22, 2017]).
5 Organizational information, as applicable in mid-2017, is drawn from the Akhuwat website or from questioning senior management.

6 Organization information procured from the head office.
7 Trainees work with Assistant Unit Managers on probation for a three-month period prior to being regularized.
8 Akhuwat's rapid expansion has coincided with periods of flooding in which the organization has worked for the rehabilitation of the affected families.
9 We evaluate these claims in Chapter 6 using information gathered from a survey.
10 This is consistent with the utilization of the preceptoral mechanism identified in Chapter 1.

References

Akhuwat. 2007. "Akhuwat: Microfinance with a Difference," 4th edition. Lahore, Friends of Akhuwat, www.akhuwat.org.pk/pdf/Akhuwat.pdf.

Government of Pakistan. 1998. "Statistics Division, Ministry of Economic Affairs and Statistics," Population Census Organization, www.statpak.gov.pk/depts/pco/statistics/pop_sex_ratio_growth_rate/pop_sex_ratio_growth_rate.html.

Harper, M., et al. 2008. *Development, Divinity and Dharma: The Role of Religion in Development Institutions and Microfinance* (Rugby, UK: Practical Action Publishing).

Munir, K. 2012. "Akhuwat: Making Microfinance Work," *Stanford Social Innovation Review*, 18, February 9.

Saqib, A. 2014. *Akhuwat ka Safar* (Lahore: Sang-e-Meel).

Zaidi, S. A. et al. 2007. "Social Impact Assessment of Microfinance Programmes," study commissioned by the European Union and Pakistan Financial Sector Reform Programme, Islamabad.

Section 2
Empirical assessment

6 Akhuwat's microcredit alternative[1]

Introduction

Akhuwat's stated vision is to attain a "poverty free society built on the principles of compassion and equity." It uses microcredit as a key tool to attain this vision. Apart from eliminating *riba* (narrowly interpreted as interest – see Chapter 8) from loan transactions, to the extent that its resources permit, Akhuwat sees its mission as a process. This includes creating empathy and social solidarity by donating back to the organization to help someone else facing similar difficulties and using borrower groups to forge community ties. It also purports to encourage self-reliance among the poor and, if possible, enhance employment by building such self-reliance (Chapter 7). The borrowers to donor principle and the emphasis on volunteerism as part of the four core guiding principles and other institutional features mentioned in the Preface and Chapter 5 are discussed further below.

After explaining our field research method and research design and sampling, we identify Akhuwat's lending methodology. We next identify the criteria we use to gauge whether Akhuwat could be viewed as a success. Our findings on all the identified criteria suggest this is overwhelmingly so, and we speculate on the causes of this success before summarizing.

Field research method

We relied on both quantitative and qualitative information primarily gathered during our fieldwork. We leaned towards qualitative research methods in order to holistically gauge and understand the organization's role in a context-specific and conceptually in-depth way. Although we rely on other sources, the most critical information has been collected from borrowers at the grassroots level based on our sample survey spanning 13 sites across the country and focus group discussions (FGDs) held at each site. Each branch serves the low-income, usually tight-knit, community immediately surrounding it, roughly in a five-mile radius. The fieldwork was thus conducted in 13 such communities. Eight of our 13 sites were in the Punjab province, two in Khyber-Pakhtunkhwa (KPK), two in Gilgit-Baltistan and one in Sindh. Our fieldwork lasted about five weeks of driving across the country from the plains of Sindh and Punjab provinces on to KPK in the Northwest and finally to Skardu, the remote district at the base of the Karakorum mountain ranges.

The Internal Review Board approval for the fieldwork was obtained through Mount Holyoke College. We initiated all respondent engagements with the recommendation for ethical survey practices of the Internal Review Board, USA, and painstakingly indicated to Akhuwat's borrowers[2] that we were independent researchers, not financially supported by the organization, and that we had no influence or say in organizational matters. Further, we assured them of confidentiality and followed appropriate procedures throughout the research to ensure this.

After the initial contact, the field staff left for the duration of the borrower interview as per our insistence to Akhuwat upper management. We used this to signal our independence from the organization and repeated this if we sensed respondents associated us with the organization and also constantly referred to Akhuwat as "they." On one occasion a respondent reproached us saying that "you ask about them as if there might be something wrong with them, and yet they don't even take water from us."

Even so, response biases are inevitable. Ideally, we as independent researchers would have preferred to talk to the borrowers in a setting that established trust and restricted external factors that could potentially influence or confound the responses. However, since we needed Akhuwat field staff to establish first contact with the borrowers, some bias could not be avoided, since the borrowers may have, by association, perceived us to be from the head office despite our best efforts to inform them otherwise. Thus this is the qualification we must begin with in cases where the beneficiary was a current borrower and intended to get another loan.

We often heard borrowers repeat to us the central messages imparted to them by the organization. The phrases "we give back to Akhuwat, so others can be helped the same way we were helped" and "we want to become givers to society instead of takers" were common responses across sites during our interviews. Whether and how deeply these messages were internalized is impossible to know fully, but we can glean to some extent from our survey data and discussions.

We also do not know if the unit managers coached respondents prior to our visit to give a positive response. However, when we encountered a disgruntled ex-borrower, whose case was closed, we inquired about the case history to get the organization's perception of the case. We were impressed by a unit manager's humility and his response that the case record should speak for itself.[3] A response bias was also possible because we were unable to secure as much access as we would have liked to ex-borrowers, which is discussed further below

On the positive side, we were amazed at the completely full access we were given to randomly selected individuals without Akhuwat staff being present during the interviews. In fact, since the perception conveyed to the borrowers was that we were "a checking team," it gave them every opportunity to freely complain in the complete confidence we assured them.

It was quite evident in the field that the daily work routine of the branch office was adversely impacted by our presence and demands, and we tried our level best to complete our work as soon as possible. We found the field staff to be very patient and cooperative. Abandoning a car/walk mode of interviewing and embracing motor bikes (riding behind unit managers) to move swiftly into and on narrow city lanes and unpaved village tracks accelerated the survey to mutual benefit. But it bears repeating that this is an organization that freely opened itself to scrutiny with complete confidence that it had nothing to hide.

Research design and sampling

Initially we requested Akhuwat to provide us with a sampling frame that would only include individuals whose loan contract with Akhuwat had ceased, i.e. those who received one or more loans but had none outstanding at the time of the interview and did not plan to get a loan in the future. Our reasons for this selection were two-fold. First, current recipients may not have had the time to fully process their interaction with Akhuwat. Second, they might be more favorably biased in their responses since they would be borrowers at the time of interview. A bias might also have been introduced by their desire for and expectation of additional loans. We thought we could get a full picture of how borrowers benefited from the loans they received and of their reflections regarding their interactions with Akhuwat once the loan contract was completed.

We confronted several problems during the pre-tests in tracing ex-borrowers and that resulted in our changing our research design. First, since there is staff turnover, the new unit managers often did not know the earlier borrowers. Second, in early 2015, the Government of Pakistan decided to block cell phone sims registered without biometric data. Many people decided not to register their biometric data, and so many old cell contacts in Akhuwat's records were unreachable. Third, some individuals migrated or passed away. Finally, we found that since ex-borrowers were no longer beholden to the organization, they were less responsive to current unit manager requests for interviews, especially since they do not know the new unit managers.[4]

We therefore decided to opt for a sampling frame which included both old and new borrowers. In retrospect, we realized that we could have oversampled ex-borrowers. However, diminishing marginal returns in securing interviews set in very fast once current borrowers had been interviewed, and we sought interviews with ex-borrowers. Spending more time per site was commensurate with higher cost per interview because of higher fixed costs such as automobile rent and hotel stay. It was also expensive in terms of the organization staff members' time because they had to trace ex-borrowers ahead of our arrival. Since our arrival virtually suspended the normal business of the branch, we had reason not to overstay our welcome despite support from the head office.

While we have explored to see, in relevant cases, if there are systematic differences in responses of borrowers and ex-borrowers, there may be response biases. The responses of ex-borrowers could vary based on whether they completed a loan cycle and did not need another one, planned to get another loan but did not have one yet or were denied an additional loan after having applied.

The sampling frame contained 47,914 respondents from 253 branches. This represents the population that we generalized to. We first randomly selected 5 percent of the branches (13 branches out of the 253 – Appendix 6.1 lists the sample distribution by branch). Given our budget, we randomly selected 1.5 percent borrowers and ex-borrowers from each branch for a total sample size of 458 respondents: 43 percent females and 57 percent males. Overall we managed to interview 267 individuals, 78 ex-borrowers, which represented a yield rate of 58.3 percent.[5] As indicated above, we explored and reported when relevant if there is a difference in response by current and ex-borrowers. We also explored gender differences in the responses. Of those interviewed, the non-response on individual questions was very limited and reported only if notable. The percentages reported are based on those responding.

We did not include a control group for selection bias because Akhuwat deliberately selects on perceived honesty, industry and entrepreneurial skills when reviewing applications and business plans. The point of this exercise is precisely to provide loans to those most likely to succeed and benefit themselves and their communities. This research is therefore not an impact assessment but a broad and qualitative institutional analysis of a particular approach to delivering microcredit in the context of others reviewed in Chapter 4.[6]

While our approach is mostly qualitative, we fielded a semi-structured questionnaire to address the research questions identified in Chapter 5

(Appendix 6.2).[7] Since our main focus in the analysis is on qualitative responses, we were comfortable with the small sample size selected based on our budget and time constraints. We had the option of hiring a field team for interviews, and that would have enabled us to secure many more interviews and hence a larger sample size. However, we both thought it better to do the interviews ourselves knowledgeable as we were about the research questions.

Our second instrument is a list of questions we used for FGDs at each of the sites (Appendix 6.3). These questions were also built around our Chapter 5 research questions and issues that were flagged during the pre-tests. In all we held 29 male and female FGDs with individuals not in our sample (three during the pre-test). The distribution by size and gender is reported as Appendix 6.4. In addition to these two instruments, we extensively interviewed head and field offices personnel for organizational information (Appendix 6.5 lists interviewees). The instruments were honed and finalized after two pre-tests on January 5–7, 2015, and again on May 11, 2015. After finalization of the instruments, the fieldwork began on May 13 in Sukkur, Sindh, and ended June 12, 2015, in Rawalpindi.

Akhuwat's lending methodology

In order to determine eligibility for loans, Akhuwat relies on a social appraisal mechanism as opposed to any kind of collateral. A social appraisal form developed for this process (Appendix 6.6 provides key details) is filled in based on a home visit to determine if indeed the household is in need of support and capable of paying back the loan. The criteria used includes details such as whether the house is owned or rented, size of household, forms of income and detailed breakdown of total monthly savings and expenses. If Akhuwat concludes the family should be able to save, the loan could be denied. Similarly, a steady job would generally disqualify a loan applicant. Likewise, the ability to pay back and potential responsible behavior is also gauged by assessing the person's standing in the community through inquiries.

Loans are in principle available to all poor potential entrepreneurs, but Akhuwat selects on the perceived goodness as a community member and personal industry. A household member who is tardy with installments does not necessarily tar the household if they deem another individual in the same household to be worthy. Thus in one case a son defaulted, but the mother's loan application was accepted because the branch office was persuaded that she herself was a responsible person. This enabled the household business (store) to thrive despite the son's loan request having been denied.

Loans are sequential, starting with a small loan, without a limit to the numbers of loans individuals may secure. There is however an upper limit

80　*Empirical assessment*

on loan size. The largest size available for an entrepreneurial loan was capped at Rs. 50,000 in 2016. Though a lot of beneficiaries feel the loan size is too small, the underlying philosophy is to gradually build household prosperity, self-sufficiency and independence while minimizing debt burden. Thus in addition to being interest free, the small size of the loans along with small repayment installment sizes and an extended repayment period have been institutionalized to maintain payback ease. If they are doing well and want to borrow more to enhance the size of the business, this is encouraged. Prior to each loan, there is a fresh business plan appraisal (Appendix 6.7 provides details).

The business plan appraisal is a rough balance sheet filled in by the branch staff based on discussions with the borrower and visits to the site of the enterprise (where relevant) for which the loan is to be utilized or a sighting of the asset like a rickshaw or cart. The idea is to assess if the business is running successfully, if it is on-going, or likely to succeed if it is a new one. The appraisal tallies fixed costs, inventory costs, variable costs and revenue generated. More will be said about Akhuwat's lending methodology in context as we report on our findings.

Evaluating success

In Chapter 5 we access success using statistics on conventional indicators such as growth of branches, beneficiaries, recovery rates, donations and credit pool. These statistics are reported in Appendices 5.1–5–3.

Imitation in the private sector is often viewed as a marker of business success. The same could be deemed to be the case in the civil society sector. Many individuals and organizations have in the short period of Akhuwat's existence contacted it to replicate its approach to microcredit, and the organization has encouraged such replication with technical assistance. Appendix 5.5 lists organizations that have adopted Akhuwat's lending philosophy and methods. Another criterion of success is how it is being viewed by the competition, and we will report what we were able to glean in this regard during fieldwork.

We think that other criteria of success are more important than the ones listed above. In this chapter we evaluate Akhuwat's success based on beneficiary perceptions. If those that Akhuwat purports to serve are satisfied on various counts with the service that the organization claims to deliver, then it could indeed be deemed to be a success.

Even more important in assessing an organization is exploring whether or not it attains its vision and mission as encapsulated in its founding documents. In this chapter we assess how successful it is in attaining its stated vision, and in Chapter 7 we assess whether or not it is successful in promoting self-entrepreneurship, a core element in its mission statement. In Chapter 7 we also assess success based on the macroeconomic impacts Akhuwat is already beginning to have and by using the "voice" of the borrowers concerning their enterprises.

In this chapter, we also use survey responses to evaluate Akhuwat's claims of addressing the critiques and shortcomings of conventional microcredit identified in Chapter 5, and this is central among our research questions. Last but not least, we evaluate Akhuwat's success in terms of our working definition of altruism as defined in Chapter 2. This is critical since Akhuwat claims to have built its organization around this core concept and it is the conceptual framework that drove this research.

We think that such a holistic institutional assessment criteria has more strengths than weaknesses and is in many ways superior to conventional impact assessments. We highlight in Appendix 7.1 the intractable problems of conventional impact assessments including those based on RCTs.

Findings: background

Just over nine-tenths of the borrowers had heard of Akhuwat by word of mouth, 8 percent from a posted advertisement and the rest from an Akhuwat representative.[8] Over half (54 percent) of the respondents said they had no borrowing option prior to Akhuwat, and many said that their business would have suffered or not flourished without this option. Over a quarter (26 percent) said they secured a loan from a bank or others including an interest-based loan from a financial NGO. Five percent said they had engaged in a ROSCA (Rotating Saving and Credit Association known locally as a Committee – see below and Appendix 6.8), and the same percentage said they would have borrowed from family, while a slightly lower percentage said they would have borrowed from a friend.

Over a third of those who responded (36 percent) said they had been approached by another interest-based financial NGO. More than two-thirds did not opt for such a loan, and 86 percent of them said they wanted to avoid interest even though they needed a loan. Only six of the 24 respondents who accepted an interest-based loan rated it as a positive experience.

Thirty percent of respondents were ex-borrowers (80). About 90 percent of them responded to the question of why they had stopped taking a loan, and 27 percent of them (20) said it was Akhuwat's decision to deny them another loan. Being tardy was cited as the main reason for Akhuwat's denial of a repeat loan.

About a third said they did not need another loan, and 12 percent said they were in the process of applying for another loan. Only 7 percent said they did not apply for another loan because they had difficulty paying off the first one, and only 4 percent said that difficulty in finding a group to secure a loan was a hindrance (see below). Interestingly while the suggestion of increasing the loan size occurred with the second largest frequency (Appendix 8.2), only 5 percent of ex-borrowers mentioned "the amount being too small" as a reason for not applying for another loan.

Findings: is Akhuwat a successful organization?

We addressed some aspects of this issue based on summary statistics reported in Chapter 5 appendices, and on that score the organization is overwhelmingly successful. Loan officers and other staff members informed us that Akhuwat's presence in a locality results in a decline in the business of money lenders, banks and interest-based microfinance organizations which often complain, move out of the area or reduce their interest rate.[9] Beating the competition and enabling replication too could be considered markers of success. However, more important is evaluating Akhuwat's success based on borrower satisfaction, on whether it is attaining its vision successfully and on addressing the shortcomings of conventional microcredit as it claims.

Beneficiary satisfaction

We asked respondents to rate their overall level of satisfaction with the organization (1 to 5, with 5 as maximum). A high 87 percent rated the organization as 5, and another 7 percent rate it as 4. As expected, the positive evaluation was somewhat higher for current borrowers compared to ex-borrowers. For the former, the high or very high level of satisfaction was expressed by 97 percent of the respondents while for the latter it was 92 percent.

There was virtually an identical high level of satisfaction expressed with the simplicity of Akhuwat's procedures (89 percent for 5 and 8 percent for 4) with no difference evident in the responses of current and ex-borrowers. For current borrowers the responses were 95 percent for 5 or 4 (91 percent for 5 and 4 percent for 4) and for ex-borrowers it was 94 percent for 5 or 4 (85 percent for 5 and 9 percent for 4).

Is Akhuwat attaining its vision?

An important question for us is whether Akhuwat is attaining its vision of inducing empathy and social solidarity. Akhuwat advocates that those who have been assisted should help others even if in a small way depending on their means. Those who attain self-sufficiency or prosperity could donate more than others. The mechanism for attaining this vision of social solidarity is thus soliciting donations through their borrowers to donor advocacy. While these donations are intended to be entirely voluntary, the method employed in receiving donations suggests that staff and peer pressure might be at play.[10] The donations are not anonymous in that they are given publically in the field office and a receipt is provided for the donation. While the receipt provides some level of assurance of records being maintained and hence that the funds collected are not misused, Islam prefers charitable donations to be anonymous (Chapter 2). Many borrowers during interviews and group discussions quoted the common cultural saying in this regard that "the left hand should not know what the right is doing." Others however noted that the receipt ensured their donations reached the organization when they sent them through a group member who collectively submitted the group's installments.

Ninety-six percent of the respondents donated, but more important was the reason why and whether the expressed motivation was consistent with the working definitions of altruism identified in Chapter 2. Over half of the responses (53 percent) suggested the purist form of humanitarian motivation, i.e. they were giving to help others. Over a third (35 percent) gave in the name of God, but here too it was because God prescribes giving to help the poor. Several said that giving for God or for others is the same and cast doubt on the validity of our categories. One respondent said we are "vessels for God's work," which means helping others.

At least 9 percent were recorded to have specifically mentioned that they gave to reciprocate, i.e. to "help because they were helped," but this is an overlapping category with the first one, i.e. "to help others." Giving for the mosque (10 percent) is a traditional form of charity. Perhaps one could rule out as altruistic givers the 3 percent of respondents that suggested they were simply following the organization's instructions.

Notwithstanding the generous response from borrowers, 43 percent did not approve of the collection method, though 44 percent did and 13 percent were indifferent. Of those who did not approve and indicated why, 97 percent said this was because the collection method was too public. To a direct question on the method of donation collection, 54 percent expressed a preference for anonymous collection.

Evaluating claims

Social harmony

As earlier stated, for Akhuwat microcredit is a means to an end. The end is social change based on a change in social attitudes. Thus, Akhuwat claims

84 Empirical assessment

that compared to other microcredit organizations, it creates social harmony based on social solidarity. The concept behind giving group loans is that group members should help each other.[11] In the best of circumstances, if one member is unable to muster the resources for an installment, the others should pool resources as a means of temporary support for the member in difficulty. They should also alert each other regarding payments due. Payments are only accepted for the whole group and not on an individual basis, and hence the group is jointly responsible. Therefore one group member can collectively deposit installments for the entire group, which reduces transaction costs for the borrower in terms of trips to the branch. If there is a delayed payment, the field staff calls the individual that is tardy but also uses the group to apply peer group pressure. Since the group is jointly liable, a delay in payments spoils the collective group record, and the worst-case scenario is that the whole group is denied repeat loans. This collective punishment is similar to other microcredit organizations, and the outcome can be an erosion of social capital.

There was however a great deal of willingness among respondents across the board to concede that any follow-up on the part of the organization to collect loans was entirely justified since they need to protect their funds for loans to others. Further, there was an acknowledgment, as taught by the organization, that if they repay on time, others got credit on time and that this was part of being good citizens.

We explored the extent to which individuals may have internalized Akhuwat's social philosophy based on responses to several questions.

If social solidarity was internalized as a value based on organizational advocacy, we would expect most borrowers to endorse group lending and prefer group loans to individual loans. Over nine-tenths of the current borrowers (91 percent) and about four-fifths of ex-borrowers (78 percent) thought the group experience was positive. Females (92 percent) were more likely than males (84 percent) to view group loans as working well for them. Those who found the experience to be positive cited how all the group members were timely and honest and they liked the mutual support.

The main reasons identified for the negative experience of operating in a group was peer group pressure, not finding peers to be responsible or trouble forming a group. As per the organization's rules, a group cannot be formed by members of the same household. However, the group members must also not reside beyond two streets away. This requirement was mentioned as creating difficulty in group formation especially for borrowers in older branches where most potential borrowers were already in groups.

Notwithstanding the reported positive group experience, more than half (56 percent) said they would prefer an individual to a group loan, 13 percent were indifferent, while only 31 percent said they preferred a group loan. The notable difference between current and ex-borrowers is that while 35 percent of current borrowers preferred the group loan, only 21 percent of ex-borrowers expressed such a preference, and so Akhuwat's advocacy might have become more effective over time. Again, notwithstanding the more positive experience of groups claimed by females, 52 percent of them still preferred individual over group loans, while at 58 percent this preference was higher among males.

The main reasons for preferring individual loans was that respondents wanted to avoid the hassle of finding a group, and once found operating in one in terms of establishing trust, coordinating repayments, and being held accountable for others. Whether this finding suggests that individualism is the human condition or whether this human trait is created by operating in a market system is difficult to say based on this limited evidence. In any case, Akhuwat has a struggle on its hands in engineering the kind of social solidarity it envisions as a preferred human condition. It has made progress in this regard because those who preferred a group loan, though in a minority, found it to be less burdensome and more convenient to work with others and found the social solidarity to be a blessing.

Household harmony

Akhuwat claims that unlike other microcredit programs criticized for generating household tension (see Chapter 5), it nurtures household harmony. On a direct question about whether the loan from Akhuwat created any tension in the household, 96 percent of the women and 85 percent of the men said no. Women had particular reason to be satisfied since virtually all reported that they used the funds according to their own wishes. Only **one** woman reported that the funds were used by her husband against her wishes. The individual narratives in Chapter 7 indicate this may be an understatement, but the narratives also demonstrate that the wives and husbands worked as a team, and we did not confront a single case of acrimony in relation to the loans. In this regard, Akhuwat's ideological predilection of viewing the household as an integrated unit appears well founded.[12]

Household harmony can be created by transparency in the solicitation and use of funds. Akhuwat has introduced an innovation by requiring that all loan agreements need to be signed by a household member in addition to the person soliciting and receiving the loan. Sixty-nine percent of the women but only 57 percent of the men approved of co-signing the loans while 21 percent of the women and 28 percent of the men opposed the co-signing while the rest were indifferent.

Most women who opposed co-signing mentioned issues such as the transaction costs associated with obtaining a signature from male family members because it is difficult to convince them to go the branch during working hours, particularly if they work out of town. The reasons cited by men were more patriarchal, with some mentioning that the branch is not a place for women to go to or that it is embarrassing to go and publicly obtain a loan with your wife. Once again, more work is needed to get reluctant borrowers, particularly men, on board to appreciate this practice.

Low overheads

This claim bears out in what we saw in the field and in the numbers. Branch offices have one table with cushions around it on the floor, a file cabinet or a steel cupboard. While area offices have chairs for data entry, they too are simple and austere. Despite being a cash business, they do not hire security guards and have had no incidents of theft. Their response to our query in this regard was that they rely on community goodwill.

Staff behavior

One of Akhuwat's claims is that unlike other microcredit organizations its staff conduct is exemplary. Borrowers were asked to rate staff conduct from 1 to 5 with 1 as very poor and 5 as very good. Eighty-nine percent rated staff conduct as very good, and another 9 percent rated it as good. Among ex-borrowers, the percentages were 83 percent and 10 percent respectively. Thus, there is strong support for Akhuwat's claim regarding the polite conduct of its field staff members.

Our field observations and interactions and group discussions also revealed that Akhuwat is indeed exemplary in terms of the gracious, patient, polite behavior of the field staff. As narrated by a unit manager, Dr. Saqib's message is that "it is only the goodness of a person that counts and not their religion, sect, caste, creed, race or gender." As the numbers concerning staff behavior above show, the message regarding treating all people well appears to have been internalized by the staff.[13]

A common expression used to describe the staff behavior was that "they don't even take water when they visit our house," which implies how cognizant the staff is of vulnerable loan-bearing families and the potential burden a loan can impose. The organization's emphasis and commitment to staff training and careful and context-specific approach was very evident during our fieldwork.

Loan treadmill and expansion

Akhuwat has good reason to claim that it does not put borrowers on a loan treadmill. While it has an incentive to give more and bigger loans since it collects a service charge on public funds that are part of its credit pool (Chapter 8), there is no evidence that it acts on that incentive. In fact, as documented in Chapter 8, the most frequently expressed suggestion from borrowers is that the loan size should be bigger. Akhuwat gradually increases loan size based on demonstrated effective use of the first loan, evidence of continued need, and an assessment of sound future business plans to ensure that borrowers are on a path to self-sufficiency and will not have difficulty with repayment of installments. It assesses its success on borrowers graduating and not needing additional loans, and this is the antithesis of a business model that hinges on giving more and bigger loans. Finally, it closely monitors the use of funds to ensure appropriate and effective use (Chapter 7).

Agent for neo-liberalism?

As indicated in Chapter 4, many microfinance institutions (MFIs) are accused of being agents of neo-liberalism such that basic human needs are no longer provided by the state but rather an individual responsibility.[14] Akhuwat certainly believes in self-reliance as part of its mission statement. Initially, its vision was a credit pool for on-lending built entirely on civil society philanthropy, and this distinguished it from other donor funded MFIs. Of late, it can be characterized as a public-private partnership because on the liability side of its balance sheet (Chapter 8) the bulk of its credit pool is derived from public lending for enhancing small-scale enterprise employment. It believes that creating livelihoods is the best method of meeting human needs.

Akhuwat has also recently accepted a modest grant from a foreign donor (Care International, UK) for the credit pool to be given out on a revolving fund basis. However it has moved the discourse beyond neo-liberal individualism, or at least attempted to shield communities from intrusive market individualism, by its emphasis on *bhaichara* or brotherhood.

Focus group findings: the borrower's voice

We relate edited versions of some selected comments from our notes and then summarize some of the main themes that came up during the FGDs. During one FGD, everyone agreed that Akhuwat treated them well and with respect on an individual level. A woman in the group particularly appreciated that women are referred to as "*behen*" (sister) or "*baji*" (older sister) and spoken to with respect. Another person mentioned that that they liked the fact that Akhuwat's perspective is that "you are not a customer, you are a family member."

In a male FGD, Akhuwat was compared to a standard MFI operating in the area. We were struck with the repetition of the operational critique of conventional microcredit organizations that we documented in Chapter 4. They considered the MFI to be not only interest based, which they disapproved of for religious reasons, but also predatory in their method of installment collections (including forcibly appropriating durable goods like TVs). The field staff members of these organizations were viewed as preemptory and rude. By contrast, they found Akhuwat staff to be helpful and courteous. Again, many remarked that they would not even accept a glass of water when making field visits as a symbol of not being exploitative of clients being served.

One member of the group wondered if his friend's second loan approval was rejected because he made no "voluntary" donations. While it was left unsaid, group members wondered if the voluntary donations were indeed a form of implicit interest. They felt that in the spirit of charitable donations prescribed by scripture, these donations should be anonymous and undocumented and only then could they be deemed voluntary.

In the vast majority of FGDs, respondents noted that the field staff does not reprimand with hostility but explained that repeated late payments could potentially affect a borrower's record and hinder the success of future loan applications. Their often repeated message was that late payments erode trust and also hinder the organization's ability to help others if loans are not returned in a timely manner. It was clear that Akhuwat's message was well internalized across the board.

Some common themes that came up as in the survey responses were kudos for Akhuwat for providing an interest-free option that saves them from the bane of interest-based transactions, praise for the exceptional field staff, and a high level of satisfaction with how the organization treats them and responds to their problems if any and with its simple procedures. There was unanimity on the latter issues but not so on other issues such as: loan size is too small; donations should not be collected publically; they should be able to opt for an individual loan because group loans undermine social capital.

In the female FGDs, the unique challenges pertaining to women were highlighted, especially with regard to the use of the mosque for loan disbursements. Some women liked that disbursement ceremonies were held at mosques "because it strengthened their religion." Others, across different sites, noted it became a moral dilemma for them at times since it is considered sinful to enter mosques in a 'state of un-cleanliness' (while menstruating) but they still had to attend.

During disbursements, women are expected to be seated next to men in large segregated groups in the religious space. One FGD participant noted "we are just on the side in the mosque," making evident a sense of marginalization.

We were also made aware from FGDs across the country that in this, as in other regards, Akhuwat's policy is context specific. Occupying a common space, even if segregated, can be viewed as highly offensive in some ethnic contexts. For example, in Mardan, KPK, where patriarchal cultural norms are a lot stricter, a woman mentioned that "we are *Pathan* – we take offence" at the notion of utilizing mosques for common yet segregated disbursement ceremonies. So while common but segregated disbursements occurred in many sites such as Khairpur, Sindh or in the church in Islamabad, this was not the case in KPK.

While most women said that a husband's permission is important and so approved of co-signed loans, others, across different sites, asserted that the loan application process becomes very tedious because of this stipulation. At one FGD it was mentioned that "it is tough trying to get the husband to go to the branch when he is on daily wages." At another it was noted that they discontinued the practice of accepting other female members of the household's co-signing the loan: "Why don't they accept daughters' signatures anymore? She has an identification card so why not? Mother-daughter signatures should be accepted." At the Skardu site, women in the FGD unanimously abhorred this requirement saying that most of their husbands work out of town and questioned what might happen if they are divorced or widowed.

Many female respondents agreed that group loans were useful and created mutual support. One respondent said that it "facilitated a sisterhood" amongst the group members. Others noted that the option of individual loans should be there in cases a group cannot be formed.[15]

Explaining success

Over all we conclude from the findings reported in the last section that Akhuwat at the moment represents a success story. It is expanding rapidly based on donations and fund raising, attaining its vision (and mission, Chapter 7), meeting conventional microcredit success criteria, entertaining requests for replication, beating the competition, satisfying its borrowers and meeting most of its claims in addressing the shortcomings of conventional microfinance. While our research method does not enable us to rigorously identify the causal factors, our fieldwork nonetheless enables us to speculate on what some of the institutional and organizational causes of success might be.

It is clear from borrower perceptions that the organization is viewed by both current and ex-borrowers as an overwhelming success.[16] We coded open-ended responses on why there was such a favorable rating. Since the respondents often provided multiple reasons, we coded the first reason provided as the one that they viewed as most important.

Twenty-eight percent attributed the high rating to various aspects of organizational behavior such as the politeness of the staff. A quarter rated them highly due to the help they got, and another fifth due to the help the organization provides to the poor. Since they viewed themselves as poor, there is an overlap between the latter two responses. Only 1 percent explicitly stated interest-free loans as a reason for the high rating, but once again this merged with personal help and help for the poor more broadly. Several mentioned small loan sizes and small and extended repayment installments were very welcome because they facilitated repayments.

We speculate on possible causes of borrower satisfaction with the organization based on our field observations. First, the leadership of Akhuwat has brilliantly tapped into a receptive audience and found a perfect niche. The leadership is deeply committed to the religious ban on *riba*, and the popular sentiment against this is also broad and deep (survey results). Hence the demand for their loans is vast even though knowledge of Akhuwat is mostly spread by word of mouth. The ability to access interest-free loans unleashes enormous goodwill.

Second, there is the wide spread respect for Dr. Amjad Saqib (a medical doctor fondly referred to as Dr. Sahib by the staff), the organization's co-founder, chairman and executive director. During our interview with him, he came across as humble, kind and charismatic and completely willing to engage. He greets visitors by sitting on a carpeted floor with cushions along part of the wall, much as is the case in the field offices, so that the organizational culture of simplicity, cleanliness, non-hierarchy and frugality pervades across the board. He has no climate control in his office even in a higher floor office in extreme heat in a very hot city. The multi-functionality of the office is evocative of the policy thoughtfulness one can witness in the field.

He is widely venerated by the staff but aware that the cult of personality could damage the sustainability of the organization and hence the leadership (the Board of Directors and executive director) has put systems into place that are easily replicable and structurally self-sustaining.[17] However, the above-mentioned veneration is helping with the establishment and expansion of the organization. He interacts with staff at all levels, and one mid-level staff member noted that engaging with him changes one's psyche forever in the direction of wanting to do good works.

He showed every indication of being capable of being a Muhammad Yunus[18] and would probably have a much larger profile if the Western world was not hostile and suspicious of Islam, a suspicion shared at least by Western-oriented elites in Pakistan. Further, opposing interest, which is so central to the capitalist market economy, means he may face an uphill battle for broader acceptance in the corridors of global power notwithstanding his organization's successes in poverty alleviation.[19] But the leadership seems unconcerned about a profile and believes they are quietly doing "good work" as enjoined by their religion. In this case, it is to make self-sufficient as many poor people as their resources can reach.

As indicated in the Preface and Chapter 5, all loan distribution meetings begin with a talk by a religious scholar regarding the Prophet Muhammad's endorsement of commerce and of being self-sufficient. Dr. Saqib, as he documents in his book (2014), was taught a lesson by a self-respecting poor woman who refused his suggestions of taking an interest-based loan from a development NGO. Instead, she asked for and accepted an offer of an interest-free loan from Dr. Saqib's friend, and this *Qarz-e-Hassn* (interest-free loan or beautiful loan)[20] was duly paid back as the woman was enabled to stand on her own feet. This woman's insistence on an interest-free loan consistent with her religious principles and her subsequent self-sufficiency taught the moving force and co-founder of Akhuwat the lesson that became his source of inspiration and subsequently that of many of his followers.[21]

As a member of senior management in a quasi-government rural support program engaged in conventional microfinance, he had felt dissatisfied and here was a way out. It started with a small revolving fund based on voluntary contributions from a group of friends in 2001.[22] Based on his humility, simplicity, and discipline, he has inspired his staff and virtually unleashed a social movement of individuals inspired to do good by his example. Resultantly, travelling around the country and looking at the work of the branches, the groundswell of popular support at the grassroots level was akin to the onset of a quiet social revolution.

This leads to the third reason for the success of this organization, and that is the discipline that permeates the whole organization. The operational similarity at the branch level across the country was amazing, suggesting that they have perfected the ability to replicate their model when expanding to new areas. The widely shared ideology, premised on self-reflection and personal accountability and also veneration of the CEO resolves the principle-agent problem and explains the high level of discipline. In this case the ED, Board of Directors and Steering Committees are the principal. The field staff is the agent implementing the principal's vision. The principal's objective is attained due to the high level of staff motivation and hence without the principal having to incur many costs entailed in extensive monitoring or in providing incentives for getting the desired result.

While we sensed that some staff members were for the most part doing a *job*, particularly in the big cities, for most achieving the organization's vision was a moral crusade. There may well be discordance in the enlightened

92 Empirical assessment

vision evident from Dr. Saqib's writings and teachings and of the attitude of some field staff members who may not be quite as enlightened in terms of viewing religion as a vehicle for harnessing community solidarity and social justice. In conversation with field staff members, we gauged that many of them simply share the vision of removing interest and the curse of the social exploitation that it represents to them because of religious doctrine.

The field staff work with virtual military efficiency. They reach the office by 8:30 am, clean the office themselves (rather than use hired cleaners, which would be possible because labor is cheap), set up and are ready for business by 9:00 am. Many of the staff members have foregone much higher salaries to work for an organization that they believe is doing good work and identify with what they believe to be a social movement to attain the organizational mission of creating social solidarity (*bhaichara*). Thus they derive a high degree of job satisfaction in doing God's work and serving the people "*khidmat -e-khalq*." One unit manager said "we are God's soldiers for eliminating the exploitation of interest," and others saw it as a win-win "because we are doing 'good work' and getting paid for it." Thus, the grassroots staff, with a few exceptions, is highly dedicated, motivated and committed.

However, the organization does not merely rely on the dedication of the field staff and also uses conventional good management practices of initial and continued staff training, careful monitoring (surprise checks and audits), rewarding performance, creating a career path and promoting from within the organization based on perceived honesty and observed hard work and effectiveness (Human Resource Manual). Ultimately an organization and leadership is judged by the results at the grassroots level and by all indicators based on perceptions and beneficiary responses they have done remarkably well so far.[23]

While Akhuwat has generated a very positive response from the borrowers it serves and this has generated an impressive recovery rate (see Appendix 5.1), it also uses non-conventional and conventional methods to ensure the sustainability of its credit pool.[24] The non-conventional method is ideological and relies on the religiosity of its borrowers. Getting a loan in a mosque is perceived as a pact with God and not lightly repudiated – a form of induced moral self-policing. However, repeat loans and peer group pressure, as explained above, are the more conventional mechanisms. Giving the loan to the household rather than the individual not only assures that all in the family know of the loan, and this is broadly approved of, but it also holds the household co-signer (generally a spouse) liable. Akhuwat arrived at a winning formula based on trial and error. This includes pragmatism as well as advocacy and showing religiosity in deeds rather than merely words to generate goodwill.

Finally, in keeping with its broader modus operandi, Akhuwat has also wisely tapped into local financial tradition. Its loan product is very similar to ROSCA (*committee* in local parlance, Appendix 6.8), which is widely used and well understood, particularly by the kind of poor borrowers Akhuwat serves. The similarities of a *committee* with the Akhuwat loan product are that a lump sum is received, no interest is due, and monthly installments need to be paid. The difference is that all meeting Akhuwat's stringent loan criteria get first draw. Another difference is that Akhuwat has eased repayments by stretching out the time over which the installments have to be paid back.[25] Finally, there is an expectation of a modest donation in the case of an Akhuwat loan.

In both cases peer group pressure applies to induce loan repayment. However, in the case of ROSCAs it is very intense and defaults are rare since individuals risk getting blackballed with regard to future *committees* and possibly hurt psychologically, emotionally or physically. In Akhuwat's case, late installments initially result in gentle pressure from the field staff based on the preceptoral mechanism (appeal to a moral code of conduct based on religious teachings – see Chapter 1). However, the group guarantors can be used to apply pressure and defaulters know they have no possibility of ever getting a repeat loan.

Summary

Based on various criteria identified in this chapter, we view Akhuwat to be a highly successful organization and one that is, for the most part, attaining its vision. In terms of borrower's perceptions, 97 percent of current borrowers and 92 percent of ex-borrowers rated their overall satisfaction with Akhuwat as very good or good. Borrowers view it as a great success because it helps the poor or helped them or because of how it conducts itself.

Organizationally we consider its success to be premised on the charisma of the founder and his humility, simplicity and leadership by example. These traits have infused passion and dedication in the field staff that identifies with the Akhuwat vision of building a poverty-free society based on the principles of compassion, empathy, equity and self-reliance. Many view the time they spend working for Akhuwat as an opportunity whereby they are being paid to do "good works." Others who the organization views as exceptional for their honesty, hard work and dedication opt for a career path crafted by the organization.

Akhuwat also uses conventional organizational principles to put systems in place to ensure transparency, accountability, fair assessment, efficiency and effectiveness.

Akhuwat views itself as a microcredit organization with a difference and also one that has developed a methodology that enables it to avoid the pitfalls of conventional microcredit. This is in addition to its claim that it promotes social solidarity by encouraging altruism. While an impressive percentage of total borrowers give back to help others by contributing to the organization's revolving fund, we were not entirely persuaded that the method that Akhuwat has developed to promote giving conforms to altruistic giving as identified in Chapter 2.

In the past Akhuwat had posted collection boxes so that the giving could be entirely anonymous. However, the needs of accountability altered the method to giving publically in the office and issuing a receipt to the donors. This is reassuring to 44 percent of the borrowers who expressed a preference for some accountability. However, 43 percent disapproved of this method of soliciting borrower donations. The main reasons for this disapproval were that the donations were too public and that they were not consistent with a preference for anonymous giving in Islam. Fifty-four percent expressed a preference for anonymous giving.

We also explored the other Akhuwat claims, and overall we evaluate it to have delivered on its claims on most counts. The organization certainly keeps its overheads very low as it claims by practicing extreme simplicity. The staff was perceived to be helpful, courteous, and polite, and 89 percent rated them as very good and another 9 percent as good. Finally, since Akhuwat does not collect interest but only a modest administrative fee, it claims that it has no incentive to get its borrowers on a loan treadmill. Instead, it takes pride in those who are able to succeed in their business, create jobs and donate so that others can follow in their footsteps. Given its conservative approach to giving loans, despite the service fee it can charge on loans given on public donations to its credit pool, there is evidence to support its claims of preventing indebtedness and creating self-sufficiency. We explore these issues further in Chapters 7 and 8.

Akhuwat finesses the feminist critique. Feminist scholars have urged looking within the black box referred to as the household in economics since that is also where gender discrimination and violence against women occur. Akhuwat comes at this issue with an ideological lens, insisting that social stability is premised on household unity. This may not hold in practice in male-dominated societies, and gender oppression cannot be ruled out by wishful thinking. Akhuwat structures incentives to minimize gender conflict by giving the loan to the household rather than an individual. Even though we tried to single out individual beneficiary experience, the response invariably concerned the well-being of the household. Ninety-six percent of the women and 88 percent of the men reported no household tension resulted from the loans. Thus it appears that Akhuwat is able to build on and reinforce household harmony.

Appendix 6.1

Sample distribution by branch

Branch Name	Frequency	Percent	Cumulative
Arya Mohalla	106	23.14	23.14
Badar Colony	68	14.85	37.99
Bhulwal	55	12.01	50.00
Chishtian	40	8.73	58.73
Gambha	14	3.06	61.79
Mansehra	14	3.06	64.85
Nankana Sahib	26	5.68	70.52
Pasroor	24	5.24	75.76
Sahiwal-2	28	6.11	81.88
Shakargarh	19	4.15	86.03
Sikardu	23	5.02	91.05
Sukhar-1	27	5.9	96.94
Takht Bhai	14	3.06	100.00
Total	**458**	**100.00**	**100.00**

Appendix 6.2
Structured questionnaire

Background

Branch:	Female................................01
	Male....................................02
Akhuwat ID	**Date of interview:** ___/___/___
	Interviewer code

QNo	Question	Responses
Q1	How did you hear about Akhuwat?	Word of mouth ....01 Akhuwat representative ....02 Advertisement ....03 Other, specify
Q2	Other than Akhuwat, what were your options?	Borrowed from family ....01 Borrowed from friend ....02 Other, specify
Q3	Have you been approached by other NGOs/banks to take a loan?	Yes ....01 No 02
Q4	If so, what was your response?	Accepted ....01 Rejected 02
Q5	If rejected, why?	

(Continued)

QNo	Question	Responses
Q6	If accepted, how do you rate that experience from 1 to 5?	Very poor ...... 01 Poor .... 02 Fair .... 03 Good .... 04 Very good 05
Q7	If accepted, at what rate?	%
Q8	Tell us about your microcredit experience (loans taken and what you have done with them). Probe to get the full picture.	

Q9	Loan details?		
	#	Amount	Date
	1........01		
	2........02		
	3........03		
	4........04		
	5........05		

Q10 Are you still taking loans?

Yes..01
No...02

Q11 If no, why did you stop taking loans?

Akhuwat's decision..........................01
Amount too small............................02
Got loan elsewhere..........................03
Did not need loan............................04
Other, specify

Q12 If response is 01, what reason did Akhuwat give?

We had taken enough loans.............01
We were tardy in returning loans.....02
We defaulted...................................03
We did not contribute enough.........04
Told to go to a bank........................05
Other, explain

(Continued)

QNo	Question	Responses
Q13	Do you plan on taking more loans?	Yes..........01 No..........02
Q14	Was the size of the last loan adequate?	Yes..........01 No..........02
Q15	If no, what would you consider an adequate size?	Amount:
Q16	What would you have done with this loan size?	Set up business..........01 Extend business..........02 For running business..........03 Paid debt..........04 Used for consumption..........05 Other, explain
Q17	What did you do with the last loan from Akhuwat?	Set up business..........01 Extend business..........02 For running business..........03 Paid debt..........04 Used for consumption..........05 Other, explain

Q18	If 02, did you first establish business with Akhuwat loan?	Yes...........01 No............02
Q19	If 01 or 02, do you think you achieved your objective?	Yes...........01 No............02 Somewhat....03
Q20	Explain, if 03.	
Q21	If no, why not?	Loan amount too small......01 Didn't know business.......02 Market was too small.......03 Other, explain
Q22	If answer 01 or 02 on Q17, is the business still functioning?	Yes...........01 No............02
Q23	If yes, how many family (*khandaan*) members are employed by your business?	

(Continued)

QNo	Question	Responses
Q24	How many non-family (*gher khandaan*) members are employed by this business?	
Q25	Do you plan to expand your business in the future?	Yes..........01 No..........02 Maybe..........03
Q26	If business failed, explain why.	No market..........01 Had to pay off authorities too much.....02 Lacked funds..........03 Family crisis..........04 Got too old..........05 Got a job..........06 Other, explain
Q27	Did you take a group loan?	Yes..........01 No..........02
Q28	If yes, did this work out well?	Yes..........01 No..........02

Q29	If yes or no, explain why.	Too much pressure from group 01
		Members not responsible 02
		Other, explain
Q30	Would you prefer individual to group loans?	Yes 01
		No 02
		Indifferent 03
Q31	If yes or no, explain why.	
Q32	Did your monthly household income improve due to loan (*andazan ghar ki amdani har mahine*)?	Yes 01
		No 02
Q33	If yes, approximately how much?	Calculate %
Q34	Have you ever been late (*deri*) in making payments (*qist*)?	Yes 01
		No 02
Q35	If yes, how often has this happened?	Once 01
		More than once 02

(Continued)

QNo	Question	Responses
Q36	If yes, what was Akhuwat's response (*rawaiyya*) in the last episode?	Let me off.............................01 Given me more time..............02 Threatened not to lend again.....03 Informed guarantor................04 Informed community ....05 Told me my record is affected......06 Other, explain
Q37	How do you repay installments?	Borrowing from family..............01 Borrowing from friends.............02 Borrowing income generated from enterprise for which the loan was taken...............................03 Husband's salary.....................04 Borrowing from another organization...05 Other, explain
Q38	Has the loan ever created any tension within the family (*khandaan/gharaanay*)?	Yes............................01 No.............................02

Yes............................01
No.............................02
[*If no, skip to SC7*]

Q39	If yes, specify the nature of the tension.	Regarding the use of funds ....01 Regarding repayments ....02 Other, explain
Q40	As a woman, do you feel you have any say in the use of the funds *(marzi)*?	Skip to Q41 if male Yes........01 No........02
Q41	Do you think loans should be co-signed?	Yes........01 No........02 Indifferent........03
Q42	If yes or no, why?	
Q43	Did you donate to Akhuwat *(chanda)*?	Yes........01 No........02
Q44	If yes, how much? (note amount and frequency to date)	

(Continued)

QNo	Question	Responses
Q45	If yes, did you approve of the collection method?	Yes....01 No....02 Indifferent....03
Q46	If no, why not?	It is public....01 Too much pressure....02 Other, explain
Q47	Was use of funds monitored by the staff at Akhuwat?	Yes....01 No....02
Q48	Rate overall from 1 to 5 if you think Akhuwat staff are polite (*pur kulus*).	Very poor....01 Poor....02 Fair....03 Good....04 Very good....05
Q49	Rate from 1 to 5 on the simplicity (*saadgi*) of procedures (*tariqa*).	Very poor....01 Poor....02 Fair....03 Good....04 Very good....05

Q50 Rate from 1 to 5 your overall satisfaction (*mutmaeen*) with the program.

Very poor 01
Poor 02
Fair 03
Good 04
Very good 05

Q51 You have responded very favorably to Akhuwat. Is it because

Loans are interest free 01
The organization staff is very polite 02
The procedures are simple 03
Other, explain

Q52 Do you have any suggestions for making Akhuwat a better organization?

Appendix 6.3
Focus group discussion questions

1. Are you satisfied overall with the way Akhuwat treats you?
2. Are you satisfied overall with the way Akhuwat responds to your problems if you have any?
3. Are you satisfied with Akhuwat procedures?
4. Tell us about late payments and how Akhuwat deals with this. Are you satisfied with the procedure?
5. Have you heard of any other microcredit organization in your community, and what do you think about it?
6. How do you feel about co-signing?
7. How do you feel about group loans? If you had an option, would you choose individual loans?
8. Why did you donate?
9. How do you feel about donations to Akhuwat? Would you prefer an alternative method in which they are anonymous?
10. How do you feel about the Shirakat (insurance) fund?
11. Were you asked to make an Eid contribution?
12. Do you have any recommendations for Akhuwat?

Appendix 6.4

Focus groups by size and gender

Branch	Female	Male
Arya Mohalla, Rawalpindi	7	6
Bhulwal	17	14
Chistian	11	6
Lahore	11	7
Manshera	6	9
Nankana	5	4
Pasrur	5	6
Sahiwal	12	5
Shakargarh	5	6
Skardu	5	7
Sukhar-I	4	3
Takht Bai	3	5

Appendix 6.5
Key informant interviews

Sukhar-I
Sarfraz Ahmad, Area Manager
Kamran Qureshi, Branch Manager
Kashif Rashid, Sukhar-I, Loan officer

Chistian
Babar Nasim, Area Manager
Saleem Tahir, Branch Manager

Sahiwal-2
Usman, Unit Manager
Kashif, Unit Manager

Lahore, Area-6
Khadim David, Branch Manager
Asim Ali, Unit Manager
Rashid Ali, Unit Manager

Nankana Sahib
Mohammed Faraz, Area Manager
Mohammed Usman, Unit Manager
Waseem Abbas, Unit Manager

Shakarpur
Naveed Akram, Senior Unit Manager
Waseem Siddiqui, Unit Manager

Pasrur
Abid Hassan, Branch Manager
Atiqullah, Unit Manager

Bhulwal
Mohammed Usman, Branch Manager
Mudasar Nazar, Assistant Branch Manager
Waqas Zia, Unit Manager
Sohail Hassan, Unit Manager
Umer Farooq, Unit Manager

Takht Bai
Zeeshan Sajid, Area Manager, Mardan
Naveed Habib, Assistant Branch Manager

Manshera-I
Mohsin Hafeez, Area Manager
Azhar Shah, Branch Manager

Skardu
Azhar Islam, Area Manager
Anwar-ul-Haque, Branch Manager
Mohammed Khan, Senior Unit Manager

Gamba
Nasir Hussain, Unit Manager

Arya Mohalla, Rawalpindi
Atif Shahzad Area Manager
Nadeem Ahmed, Area Manager

Appendix 6.6
Social appraisal forms

Social Appraisal		
Is the house owned or on rent?	*Total number of people in the household*	*Total number of men and boys*
Total number of women and girls in the household?	Number of people earning in the household	Total household income (monthly)
Source of income	Utility bills	Rent for house (monthly)
Educational expenses (monthly)	Food expenses (monthly)	Medical expenses (monthly)
Monthly savings/ Committee	Total committee	Date committee to be received on
Other expenses (monthly)	Amount of borrowed money	Total expenses (monthly)
Personal character and social behavior	Financial give and take	Any terminal illnesses

Appendix 6.7
Business appraisal form

1) **Fixed business cost**
   Item · Quantity · Current price · Total

2) **Current inventory cost**
   This month's inventory Cost · Average inventory Cost
   Item · Quantity of supply · Purchasing price · Total

3) **Variable cost**
   Item · per unit · Quantity · Total

4) **Total current income**
   Means of earning income (monthly)
   Business
   Daily wage work
   Income from rent
   Other
   Total

In the case of business expansion, please fill the following sections

5) **Items required for business expansion**
   Item · Quantity · Purchasing price · Total

6) **Income from new or expanded business**
   Total investment · Total expenses · Total income before new/expanded business · Total income (now)

Appendix 6.8
ROSCAs vs. Akhuwat's interest-free loans

Apart from welcoming interest-free loans on religious grounds and because they are such a boon, borrowers also understand them because of their similarity with community ROSCAs (rotating saving and credit associations). These are generally popular among the poor and middle classes who frequently engage in them. Sometimes rich businessmen engage in them for very large amounts. In local parlance they are referred to as 'committees.'

A committee is constituted when a group of mutual friends, acquaintances or neighbors agree to pool funds of an agreed amount. The lump sum that results is then received by the individuals who constitute the committee group based on an agreed upon criteria. Some lump sum distributions are based on the order determined by the person who organizes the committee in some cases while in other cases the payment sequence could be based on drawing lots. Sometimes some opt to be early receivers of the lump sum based on an emergency need while others see it as forced saving or saving for expenditures occurring later such as a for a daughter's wedding.

The resource pooling occurs every month until each individual in the committee has received a lump-sum. In effect, installments are paid back every month amounting to the lump sum divided by the number of committee members. For example, if someone in a committee group of ten people pooling Rs. 1,000 each (based on drawing lots) receives a lump sum of Rs. 10,000 first, the person has to pay back Rs. 1,000 every month for the next nine months in addition to the Rs. 1,000 the person put into the pot.

Notes

1 Refer to Chapter 5 for details on the Akhuwat microcredit model. We focus in this chapter on issues arising from field observations and the survey data.
2 One of our key-informants at the head office told us that there is a de-emphasis by the organization on the term 'borrowers' and 'beneficiaries' because of the inherent top-down hierarchy the terms imply. Instead they prefer to use the term 'members.' This is reflected in official organizational practice as well, since

borrower donations to Akhuwat are referred to as member donations. That notwithstanding, Akhuwat has yet to put into place the mechanisms that could turn its borrowers into members, and thus at the moment it is not a membership organization in the conventional sense.

3 The unit manager said he did not want to speak ill of anyone and encouraged us to pursue the relevant documentation in the head office.
4 It is not surprising then that ex-borrowers constituted almost all of the non-response. The only exception was Skardu and Gamba in the far North of the country. Here we arrived a few days before the Legislative Assembly elections, and many current borrowers had traveled back to home villages where they were registered to vote. In a couple of these interviews, we substituted a group member for the selected borrower.
5 We did not include ten filled-in questionnaires in the analysis and counted them among the non-respondents. We disqualified two responses in the field since our selection criteria were not met. In four cases the respondent's ID (identification) card number was not in our sample list. In another four cases, the ID was repeated, and we dropped those questionnaires. Strictly speaking, we should have dropped both cases since we could not be sure which of the two questionnaires was valid.
6 Refer to Appendix 7.1 on why we think an impact assessment of Akhuwat's loans is not possible.
7 Some of the questions we asked involved an ethical judgment. For example, by asking respondents if they are comfortable with giving in public, we may have made them aware of an issue they might not otherwise have thought of. Thus, we risked changing the social reality by studying it, a well-known dilemma in the sciences. We proceeded because several of these issues were brought up by respondents during our pre-test and because we believed ourselves to be benign social researchers who were intent on helping the organization rather than merely intent on critiquing it to score points.
8 All percentages are rounded to avoid creating the impression of precision.
9 Akhuwat at the grassroots level welcomes this, and some who would qualify for their loans, based on their stringent criteria, and are carrying interest-based loans are encouraged to use part of the loan to pay off the interest-based loan. If they have recently acquired an interest-based loan, Akhuwat suggests they apply once their loan is paid off so they do not carry the burden of two installment payments a month.
10 We confronted some level of unease with regard to the lack of anonymity in the collection of donations in the pre-test, and so for the fieldwork we designed questions to probe this issue further.
11 Akhuwat allows a fair amount of flexibility to the field offices in devising practices that work for them, and so there is variation in implementation details though not broad policy. In our sample, about three-fourths of groups had three borrowers, and another two-fifths had four.
12 This view of the household is contradicted by a more nuanced view of household dynamics such as Sen's (1990) cooperative-conflict model or the feminist literature such as for example Agarwal's conceptualization (1994).
13 The Operations Manual emphasizes the principles of *Muwakat*, including "brotherhood, care, empathy, equity, non-partisanship and sharing." Based on these principles, it emphasizes "responsiveness (to borrower queries), a "soft language and a gentle tone" and no harassment in soliciting repayments.

However, it accepts that social pressures of various kinds in various circumstances may need to be used.
14 Following North's (1990) terminology, MFIs are organizations rather than institutions.
15 Such an option is the norm so long as the borrower can find a guarantor.
16 Individuals often stopped by during field interviews, and our impression is that it is perceived by the broader public, which is aware of the program, as an overwhelming success.
17 Cult followings can have more to do with the human proclivity to follow than a leader's hegemonic inclinations.
18 The founder of Grameen Bank who, along with the organization he founded, received a Nobel Prize.
19 The IMF however has not been hostile and encouraged internal research on the subject in the mid-1980s when the Islamic Banking movement was in its inception. Many Western banks have also seized "interest-free banking" as an opportunity to serve masses of Islamic clients the world over. The one important difference between Akhuwat and the Islamic Banking movement as currently promoted is that the latter substitutes interest like alternatives for interest while Akhuwat shuns any return on its loans.
20 See the Preface for details of this story and the discussion in Chapter 2 on altruism and giving in Islam.
21 The similarity to the Grameen Bank founding story has been noted in the literature on Akhuwat (www.akhuwat.org.pk/History.asp).
22 For the organization's subsequent growth since 2001, refer to Appendix 5.2.
23 The basic hierarchical model of head office supervision of regional, area and branch office (staffed with unit managers) is very streamlined and (paraphrasing Dr. Saqib's words) enabled Akhuwat, both as an organization and social philosophy, to go to scale despite the critics contention that this would not be possible.
24 One unit manager, under strict secrecy, reported paying Rs. 4,000 on behalf of a defaulter to protect a recovery record and implicitly a job. Admittedly only one unit manager made us aware of such an issue, but nonetheless given Akhuwat's claim to being an organization that is different from others and not obsessed with high recovery rates as a marker of its success, it needs to investigate to ensure that pressure to secure high recovery rates is not jeopardizing staff well-being.
25 Here Akhuwat also differs from conventional microcredit organizations which have a smaller repayment period, with larger, often burdensome, installments.

References

Agarwal, B. 1994. *A Field of One's Own* (Cambridge: Cambridge University Press).
North, D. C. 1990. *Institutions, Institutional Change and Performance* (Cambridge: Cambridge University Press).
Saqib, A. 2014. *Akhuwat ka Safar* (Lahore: Sang-e-Meel).
Sen, A. K. 1990. "Gender and Co-Operative Conflicts," in I. Tinker (eds.), *Persistent Inequalities: Women and World Development* (New York: Oxford University Press).

7 Promoting self-sufficiency via enterprise

Introduction

Akhuwat's stated mission is to "alleviate poverty by empowering socially and economically marginalized families through interest free microfinance and by harnessing entrepreneurial potential, capacity building and social guidance." We explore in this chapter how successful the organization has been in attaining this mission statement based on survey responses, macro impacts of the organization and loan case histories. All three sections are a way of assessing the organization's success in attaining its mission, and that is the unifying theme of this chapter.

Akhuwat's lending and economic philosophy indicates faith in the competitive market system,[1] one free of market power on the buying and selling side. Such a competitive system exists at the level at which Akhuwat operates. Such a system is also consistent with Islamic economic philosophy (Udovitch, 1970). In Islamic tradition, entrepreneurship and trade is the antithesis of interest-based transactions. Fair counter-value is mutually exchanged as long as a free market prevails. Thus, Akhuwat encourages self-sufficiency via entrepreneurship and trade by encouraging self-employment for the very poor without jobs. This is one of the key messages in the sermons delivered in the mosque loan distribution ceremonies.

Based on this economic philosophy, its lending philosophy is one in which it is unobtrusive. It allows the borrower completely unhindered use of funds for the stated purpose once the staff has done their due diligence or economic appraisal. Based on a stringent social appraisal (Appendix 6.1), only the poor are meant to be assisted. Those with jobs are to be generally excluded since they already have a source of income.

The loan cycle starts very small and is structured to sequentially increase based on a good loan record. The goal is to build the individual's confidence up to the point where their business is self-sustaining and Akhuwat can move on to support others.[2] The micro-businesses that Akhuwat has

118 *Empirical assessment*

supported to date include various kinds of shops and self-employment including vending (see case studies below).

In this chapter we first evaluate Akhuwat's success in supporting self-employment in accordance with its mission statement. We turn next to an innovative business practice we discovered during fieldwork in which labor purchases its own capital with Akhuwat's assistance and contracts out both its labor and capital to businesses. Owning capital, in addition to labor mobility, increases labor's leverage. This demonstrates Akhuwat's flexibility and innovative funding to us. We move next to some macro impacts Akhuwat's presence generates on credit, labor and product markets. Finally, to provide a deeper sense of Akhuwat's work, the heart of this chapter is narratives of respondents willing to elaborate on their loan history in some detail.[3] These represent the voices of the respondents based on the notes we took as they spoke about their business experience.

Is the organization attaining its mission?[4]

We did not use the data we collected on the extent to which the income was enhanced due to the loan. We discerned that the numbers were too rough and ready, the more established businessmen evaded the questions, and since Akhuwat often supported existing micro businesses, it would be difficult to disassociate the contributions of the individual from that of the loan. Instead, we relied on a host of other questions to gauge the success of the loan and based on the responses find Akhuwat has been successful in attaining its mission statement of promoting self-sufficiency among the poor.

Over nine-tenths (91 percent) responded that the loan had contributed to a substantial increase in household income (same number that responded that the business was still active). There was no variation by gender, but current borrowers were more positive (93 percent) than ex-borrowers (87 percent).

A measure of the operational success of a microcredit organization is their ability to recover loans in a timely manner. Akhuwat coaches borrowers to set Rs. 50 or so aside each day from the business for the repayment of the installment. Many mentioned during fieldwork that this is what they did. The effectiveness of this strategy is evident from the 88 percent who responded that they exclusively paid back the loan from the earnings of their business. Others relied on this source but also drew on other sources of income such as family, friends or a day job.

Twenty-nine percent reported having been late in making payments (58 percent of them were late more than once). Akhuwat's response to tardiness was mostly mild, and in one third of the cases the respondent said they were simply let off without being chastised. In another third of the cases (29 percent), the borrower was given more time. In 14 percent of the cases, the borrower was informed that his record would be negatively impacted

Promoting self-sufficiency via enterprise 119

and more loans would not be forthcoming, while a tenth were informed that their record had been negatively impacted. Beyond warnings, Akhuwat exercises oversight during the process and 83 percent responded that field staff monitored their use of funds.

Forty-seven percent of the borrowers started the business with the funds procured from Akhuwat in their first loan. The rest supplemented their existing business with the loan. About four-fifths of borrowers responded that they fully attained their objective while 13 percent said there were somewhat successful. Only 6 percent responded that they failed completely in their objective. The main reason reported for a complete business failure was the lack of a market. The gender distribution indicates that 85 percent of females and 78 percent of the males respectively responded that they were fully successful in attaining their objective.

Most of those who responded that they had not fully attained their objective attributed this to the small size of the loan. Fifty-five percent of all respondents thought that the loan size was inadequate. About 77 percent said they would have used a loan of the desired size to expand their business, while 22 percent wanted it to set up a larger business.

The ultimate success for Akhuwat is not only sustained self-employment but also expansion to the point that the micro-business starts creating jobs for others. While Akhuwat hopes to support businesses that will thrive and create jobs in the future, at this moment it is mostly supporting self-employment. Two-thirds of the businesses had no additional family employees, a little more than a quarter had one additional family employee and only 6 percent had two or more additional family employees. Even so, about 18 percent of the businesses had taken on one or more non-family member, so while modest in scope, some jobs were generated. Over nine-tenths of the businesses (92 percent) expected to expand and almost nine-tenths of current borrowers expected to apply for a new loan from Akhuwat.

An innovative model of labor leverage

In inducing self-sufficiency, Akhuwat is encouraging an innovative model of labor-capital relations which provides more leverage for labor but also represents a win for capital.[5] We discovered in the field that because of an acute national energy shortage and the subsequent increase in electricity costs, home-based workers are resisting sub-contractors passing on the overhead costs on to them, as is common practice. A new model of labor-capital relations has evolved that gives labor more leverage in Sialkot, one of Pakistan's major export hubs of sports goods and surgical instruments.

In small towns close to Sialkot, labor commutes to work in Sialkot's factories. However, many of Akhuwat's loans are helping labor buy their own specialized machinery such as for glove cutting. The factory supplies the materials and the facility to house the machinery and so bears the overhead costs. However, labor owns the specialized machines housed in the factory and sub-contracts on piece rates. The remuneration from this model is much higher than for labor on a regular salary. It also enables labor to move with the machine to secure more lucrative contracts elsewhere.

Some macro impacts

While our focus has been on the microeconomic level, if this organization continues to expand at current rates, it can have important positive macroeconomic impacts. By reducing the surplus army of the unemployed, labor bargaining power and wages should increase. Many borrowers indicated they felt more in control of their life and labor (Case 106715 is an example below). Anecdotal evidence suggests that the competition is reducing the mark-up or interest rates and the increased product market supply should help poor consumers whose consumption pattern they cater to and more broadly stabilize prices. We found no evidence of market saturation or of the fallacy of composition (Chapter 4) since nine-tenths reported they achieved their objective and 85 percent reported their household income to have increased substantially as mentioned above.

There are also some less expected possible macroeconomic impacts. To the extent that its social philosophy of empathy and social solidarity is internalized, it might result in better practices among micro-businesses. Further, given high junior level staff turnover, Akhuwat passes on a highly trained and efficient staff on to other organizations and this represents an important economic externality conferred by the organization.

Finally imitation can be viewed as the sincerest form of flattery. In Skardu, an AKRSP (Aga Khan Rural Support Program) initiated LSO (Local Support Organizations) has started offering interest free loans.[6] The AKRSP started a microcredit bank and complained that Akhuwat was draining its business. While the LSO loans are due back in six months rather than fifteen, many women viewed them as less onerous in terms of procedural hoops they have to jump through to get a loan.

Loan case-histories

These narratives provide details on the kinds of micro-enterprises Akhuwat supports and nurtures. They demonstrate the entrepreneurial spirit of individuals embarking on self-employment. The unadulterated "voice" of respondents is often ignored in the social sciences and we did not want to be guilty of the same omission. Most readers will get the gist after a few loan histories and may want to skip the rest.

Case 103633 had known about Akhuwat for over ten years because he was a guarantor for other people who were being hounded by loan sharks.[7] Akhuwat gave them liberation loans to free them. Eventually he secured a loan to meet a personal need and used the rest to expand his corner store. Originally he sold vegetables but used the loan to expand to a general store and started earning a much higher income. He thought that the small loan size is a good idea because people can treat it as a committee loan and pay back the installments regularly.[8] He personally prefers being part of a group but thought that Akhuwat should allow people to opt for an individual loan because it is sometimes difficult to find a good group. He thought the practice of co-signing should be discontinued because those who are part of a joint family have to deal with too many stakeholders.[9]

Case 500563 said it was a blessing not to have to engage in interest transactions. She was also happy with the small loan size because then the installments are small and affordable. She said she could not afford to take the loans offered by the regular interest-based microfinance organizations operating in the area. She took a loan so her daughters could learn typing. Her husband did not return from Saudi Arabia so she was bringing up her two daughters on her own based on her salary as a teacher. At the time of the interview, she was living with her Uncle. She had a bad experience with one field staff member because of late payments. He marked her receipt in red ink and thought the field staff member should have been more accommodating because she often receives her salary late. She thought that the staff member should not have emphasized that the organization was doing her a favor because this was disrespectful. She insisted that the other staff members were good.

Case 501996 was operating a general store and took a loan to improve it. He was retired at the time of the interview and had ceased operating the store because the landlords looted it. The rent was too high in other places that he explored so he gave up the business. He said Akhuwat was a good organization and helped a lot of people and they did not charge extra fees. He said that matters improved further when they reduced the installment size and extended the repayment period. He was under the impression that he could not secure a loan for starting a new business but only for extending an existing business and so he did not seek another loan.

Case 506389 took a loan for garments and was thankful she was avoiding the sin of engaging in an interest-based transaction. She used the loan to start a home-based business of stitching and selling children's garments. This was her first business experience. She thought that the group certainly creates a sense of collective responsibility but there is also potential for individuals in the group dragging down the rest. She thought that individuals should be given the option of what kind of loan to take and in that case she would opt for an individual loan. She thought that cosigning by a spouse could be problematic because some husbands "do not like their wives getting ahead of them," and so co-signing by a brother should be an option since "a man's guarantee is necessary." She thought that handing out the loans in a mosque ceremony is not necessary since those who cheat and lie will do so anyway. "Un-cleanliness (due to menstruation) and a hundred other reasons" make it problematic for women to attend the mosque. However, getting a loan from Akhuwat is good because it is like getting a committee loan without the hassles of participating in a committee.

Case 509746 took a loan to improve his business. He originally had a cart for vending, but that was not working out well for him. With the loan he started a canteen and sold rice and tea. He planned to expand from a canteen to a hotel in due course. He said his savings increased from Rs. 100–200 to Rs. 4,000–5,000 monthly.

Case 105452 took the first loan to start a canteen. He took a second and then a third loan to expand the business. His father had an accident, and consequently his repayment got delayed. The field staff came to check and found him selling tea, *samosa* (savory), *chaat*, (savory) *roti* (like tortilla) and curry. He distributed food in offices and also had customers come and eat at the canteen. He said he wished that the whole community took loans from Akhuwat and benefitted like he did and no matter how much he praises the organization, it is not enough.[10]

Case 509299 was not a happy customer and in that regard was one of the few exceptions. We actually spoke to the mother who said she was familiar with the loan because the son was not at home. Her son took a loan from Akhuwat to buy and sell golf clubs. She said she was her son's guarantor, and hence could not apply for a loan, which was patently unfair.[11] She had several other peeves including that loans were distributed in a mosque. She said they had problems going to the mosque and this method of putting a hand on the Qur'an to express good faith "earns sin rather than merit." She said other organization field-staff were much politer; they even came to one's house and filled in the requisite forms. They also processed the payments in a week rather than waste time and make one feel obligated. She said that such organizations are justified in taking interest given the service they provide and all the work they do.[12]

Group loans also came in for criticism because she said if one person has a problem, they all get delayed, and they have to wait for the second loan until the whole group pays the installments due. Her main complaint was regarding the rudeness of the field staff. She said she was a busy person with much to do and transport is difficult to come by and was rebuked for being only 15 minutes late for her appointment. She said the branch manager was very rude, notwithstanding the name the organization goes by, so they do

Promoting self-sufficiency via enterprise 123

not practice what they preach. She said "we did not beg for charity so there was no reason for disrespecting and degrading us." Besides, they argued that "they should give bigger loans." She said she was a beautician and machinery is expensive so she needs a decent-sized loan. Finally she was bitter about the machinelike behavior of the staff and their unwillingness to accept their hospitality. "They are not machines," she complained.

Case 103936 took a loan to expand her husband's welding shop. She said that Akhuwat is as good as it gets and that in exchange they give what they can and this giving is not mandatory; they avoid an interest-based organization with a branch located on our street. She said they also preferred Akhuwat to a committee since getting funds from them was much quicker.

Case 508739 used her loan to pay off other loans. She sold imported undergarments and used part of the proceeds to cover the installments. She complained that her group was not co-operative.

Case 506521 gave the loan to her uncle who drove a taxi. She said she did not plan on taking more loans because the Uncle could not pay her back. Her husband drove a rickshaw, but business was not good. She liked going to the mosque for the Akhuwat ceremony because of the good words they spoke. She also appreciated that they did not come to her house to pester her because of the late payment.

We spoke to the wife of case 503961 who took a loan to repair his vehicle. Prior to getting his vehicle repaired, he drove someone else's taxi for a monthly income of Rs. 9,000. She did not think running their own taxi has increased their income. The loan size was too small and so they had to stretch themselves. She also complained about the rude behavior of the field staff when he came to collect a late installment. She thought he was oblivious of how much difficulty people can get into.

We spoke to the husband of case 502970. The wife took a loan for their daughter's marriage, and they plan on taking more loans for the marriage of other children. Their needs are much greater than the loan they got. He mentioned that they once paid off an installment of a group member and he was happy they did it. He said the organization was so good to them he felt they needed to be paid back in some way.

Case 108380 got a loan to expand his shop. He was pleasantly surprised to get Rs. 15,000 because he thought the starting loan was Rs. 10,000. He planned to request another loan for Rs. 25,000 next and wanted to pay off his installments early. However, he had to wait for the group members to clear their loans before a new loan could be sanctioned. He said he already paid an installment for another group member. He was nonetheless pleased because prior to his first loan his shop was not breaking even but business subsequently boomed. He attributed this blessing to the organization.

124 Empirical assessment

Case 106631 used her loan to purchase a machine for her husband's furniture business. This enabled them to save Rs. 4,000–5,000 on renting the machine. With a second loan they purchased a second machine and their business was doing well enough for them to comfortably draw on their earnings to pay for the dowry for their daughter's wedding.

Case 107181 operated a plastic business. With the loan he immediately bought three machines to expand his business. He said he initially only had two people working for him but now has ten employees. This has enabled him to concentrate on sales since his employees now work the machines. He found working with another bank so tedious that he abandoned it and was satisfied with Akhuwat.

Case 101534 took a loan to fix his son's rickshaw. While their material conditions eased during a difficult period, he said they had not lifted themselves out of poverty.

Case 106715 said they carefully researched this organization by talking to others who had taken a loan from them. In particular they wanted to make sure there were no hidden charges. They went ahead once they were assured that the organization was trustworthy. She took a loan to buy a machine for her husband who does embroidery. She said that her husband used to be an employee but is now independent.

Case 103690 used the loan to extend his shoe shop business by buying a second machine. He said he had seven apprentices working for him.

Case 100405 took a loan for a rickshaw and prior to the loan he drove for someone else. He wanted another loan and expressed anger and frustration because someone in the group defaulted. He had engaged in a fight with a group member in the neighborhood over this matter. He thought that since the organization did its due diligence, they should take the responsibility and not deny other group members their right if one of them defaulted.

Case 104169 utilized her loan to extend her stationary business. Unfortunately her business failed because too many bought on credit and did not pay up. She wanted another loan, but could not find a group to accept her for a second loan and was told by peers she was too old.

Case 100442 used her loan to buy dishes and extend her husband's tea stall business. Unfortunately her husband passed away and her home-based stone work business with a friend was not going well due to the hot season. She had requested the organization for a loan write off.

Case 106821 said her husband was a juice vendor, so she took a loan for extending the business. They had to borrow another Rs. 5,000 loan from a neighbor since they underestimated the cost. There were in a very dire state before the loan and were extremely grateful to Akhuwat for helping them out. They had been charged with tampering the electric meter and fined Rs. 40,000, and they were still paying off that sum. At one stage their condition was so miserable that her husband said "we should get rid of the kids." She broke down and was in tears when she narrated that they had no one to rely on and nothing to eat. She begged a woman in the neighborhood to form a group and matters had since improved for them.

Case 104646 needed tires for his tractor and the loan took him part way there. He said the tractor was now performing well and with his trolley he is managing to earn a good income carting stuff and is educating his children.

Case 102950 was a widow and took a loan for a beauty shop run by one of her daughters. She plans to set up a boutique next. She is a cancer patient and grateful that Akhuwat helped establish her daughter's business although she wished they provided a larger loan.

Case 101748 heard about a good institution working in the neighborhood on an interest-free basis. She took a loan to expand her husband's carpentry business. She said this was the first time we have taken a loan and since the amount was small they had no trouble making the installments.

Case 107171 took a loan to start a chicken shop. He was a laborer before and said it was difficult work and he earned about Rs. 300 per day. After setting up his own business he said he earned about Rs. 400 to Rs. 500 per day and life at home had improved.

Case 302994 took a loan to set up a beauty parlor in her home since her father did not approve of setting one up in the neighborhood. She is now supporting her two children with the income since her father died. She plans to take more loans as the business expands. She said that during the summer months business slows down and she supplements her income by taking in sewing to do at home.

Case 101092 took a loan to help get supplies for her son's garment stall as the business was struggling. She said she would much prefer an individual loan since "I can only give a guarantee for myself."

Case 106464 got a loan to buy a rickshaw on installments. His earlier job as a painter did not bring in a steady income but with a rickshaw he was able to get a steady livelihood by contracting to drop kids to school.

Case 104978 bought stitching machines and was earning Rs. 300 per day while raising her children and doing housework. Her husband is a laborer and so did not bring in a guaranteed source of income. They used a second loan to buy animals, which they kept for six months and then sold at a profit. She mentioned that a larger loan would have meant a larger profit. She intended to take more loans to buy more machines to expand her stitching business. She came across as very ambitious and was confident that Akhuwat could lead her to a better future.

Case 105639 had taken three loans and she and her husband, a farmer, were very pleased with the outcome. They had bought buffaloes and sold the milk for a regular income. They sold a calf at Eid[13] for about Rs. 50,000 to Rs. 60,000.

Case 105959 was similar in that the loan was used to buy a pair of goats. They maintain two at a time and sell the kids for a regular income supplement.

Case 108184 took a loan for her son to add to inventories. She said she was embarrassed to confess the size of the loan they took and would only accept a lakh (Rs. 100,000) in the future, which is a minimum requirement for business people like her family. She said Akhuwat loan was too small and had too many requirements.

Case 203487 bought materials for his rickshaw decoration shop with the loan. He learned the trade at Burrewala and was putting his acquired skill to good use.

Case 200245 was trying his hand simultaneously at several businesses. He got toffees from factories for wholesaling. He also packaged laundry soap with an assistant into small sachets to distribute to retailers. He was determined to expand his business and set up his own factory so that he did not have to import from other industrial cities like Multan or Faisalabad.

Case 204934 expanded his photo studio with the loan. He bought a printer and a CPU to help him process pictures for school events.

Case 208348 had a bangle business but gave that up and set up her son as a grocery bag wholesaler. She said they earned Rs. 1,000 per month and moved into a better house because of the loan.

Case 209619 said she originally wanted to get a loan for herself but refused to take an oath of good intent on the Qur'an as a requirement for the loan. She also said she had little patience for the run-around she got. Her father took a loan and got a cart. He wanted to start a wood business but was unable to succeed because of ill health. She paid off her father's installments and advised him not to try for another loan but he persisted. His group ejected him due to a lack of confidence in him and his second loan request was denied. Akhuwat's branch manager said they were willing to work with him if he could form another group.

Case 201751 took a loan to start a beauty parlor. They did not get a second loan because their earnings increased substantially. One signal for the organization was that they paid four installments early and in one go. Their objection to group loans was that people were often pressured by friends to take loans even if they do not need them.

Case 204247 secured a loan while studying for his diploma in associate engineering. He started a shuttering business with it and partly paid the fees with his earnings. He said if he got a job after completing his last semester he would not need to request another loan.

Case 204501 used the loan for his electronic repair store. He had two shops but lost one when an electric shock injured his brother. He spent much time and money trying to re-habilitate his brother with Akhuwat's help.

Case 206783 used the loan for buying equipment for his automobile repair shop. He did not think the loan was adequate because he was in a very expensive business with spare parts often costing as much as Rs. 2,000.

Case 201671 used the loan for putting a roof on his barber shop. He said he not only comfortably paid back the loan but was also able to pay back his interest-based loan to Asha (a microfinance organization). He said Akhuwat had virtually eliminated loan sharking in the community.

Case 200042 established a furniture business with his first loan. He bought hand tools to build furniture, kitchenware, doors, and windows. With his second loan he extended the business by buying specialized machinery.

Case 304221 took a loan to start a grocery store. While he had a job in the health sector, he wanted to supplement his income. He said his group members were like his brothers and they paid all installments together.

Case 300038 took a loan to buy his wife an embroidery machine for her home-based stitching business. He also said that people have virtually stopped taking interest-based loans in the area.

Case 55702 used the loan for a garment shop that the women in his household were running. He supplemented the household income by doing a job on the side.

Case 304002 took a loan to buy seeds and supplemented the amount received by borrowing from others. He said that since they receive the money in a mosque (God's house), they had to return it. The field staff visited their farm many times for checking before they agreed to give the loan.

Case 102309 used the loan to set up his cell phone shop. He said he made a profit by buying in bulk and selling at retail. He was very grateful for the Akhuwat loan that enabled him to work and continue his education. He thought he would have had to labor in a factory otherwise and that would have left him little time for his studies.

Case 106445 took a loan for his wheat business. He earned an income from it by buying and selling and also worked as a porter.

Case 102167 took a loan to buy supplies for her husband's store. Her husband did not qualify since he was over fifty.

Case 100945 was asked to join a group and she used this as an opportunity to start a business. She started buying cloth in bulk and her husband, who was a daily laborer, started selling the cloth.

Case 203387 took the loan to buy specialized machinery for her son to produce embroidery for exports. This enabled her son to work in a factory and they do not have to run up their own utility bills.

Case 205570 used his loan for a food stall he and his two brothers used to run on the side while working as laborers. With a second loan they extended the stall and were engaged in the business full time.

Case 205712 took her first loan to start a stitching business when her husband lost his job. She said that more than one breadwinner is necessary for the household. Her business was doing well and her husband had started driving a rickshaw to supplement the household income.

Case 204335 took a loan to enable her husband to become independent in his business as a car mechanic. She said he had a partner but they were constantly in conflict about who contributed more to the business.

Case 204811 was paying back her third loan taken for her clothing business that she had established eight years earlier. She charged from Rs. 1,000 to Rs. 1,200 per suit and allowed her customers to pay in installments. She sold between 15 and 18 per month and was very pleased with the state of her business and with Akhuwat for helping her prosper.

Case 206153 used the loan to start a stitching business. He said he earned about Rs. 500 to Rs. 600 daily, feels established and comfortably feeds his family.

Case 204114 said he was a wage worker but was familiar with the art of woodworking. He said a loan from Akhuwat had enabled him to start his own business which was prospering. He said if it continues to prosper he plans to take more loans to expand the business.

Case 207180 took a loan to start a corner store located next to a school. Before this loan, the husband and wife team were in the recycling business, and they still made copies from recycled material for sale at their store to school children. They supplemented their income from the store by doing daily labor when available.

Case 826887 took a loan for a shop. In the past he had difficulty meeting expenses. To compound his problems, his landlord decided to evict him, and this resulted in a loss since he had decorated the shop. Business was good after the loan he got from Akhuwat. He had invested about Rs. 6,000 to Rs. 7,000 on a counter and frame for his shop. With his second loan he bought two stitching machines for his embroidery work. He used to be a wage worker before he set up the shop with his first loan. He said he put in about Rs. 500 per day worth of labor but was paid Rs. 120 for the bloodsucking work he did.[14] After 20 years of hard work he was finally earning what he should for his efforts now that he had his own business. He made about Rs. 1,000 to Rs. 1,200 per day depending on the work he got. He was puzzled why Akhuwat had framed a rule that Christians like him need to have a Muslim in their group. He also said it was a source of tension for him when he had to worry about others.

Case 106637 took a loan to start a cell phone shop. He thought the loan size for his first loan was adequate because new business is risky. However, subsequently he wanted a bigger loan because his business was established.

Case 303686 took a loan for his business which he said was flourishing. He was able to pay the college fees for his two siblings and was also studying privately to enhance his qualifications. He said his business success had enabled him to greatly reduce his father's burden. He found the office closure at the end of every month for an audit tedious but other than that everything else worked very well.

Case 201693 was a *kari* (religious instructor) of a mosque and took a construction loan to strengthen the foundation of a *madrassa* (Islamic religious school). He had stopped taking loans because he was too busy. However, he originally had a few objections also such as the presence of women in the office and also the issuing of checks in a mosque. His friends also said that the Rs. 200 administrative fee was not permissible and the 1 percent fee for the *sharakat* or mutual support fund (see Chapter 5) was also not permissible as a debt instrument.[15] However, recently he had seen a program on television in which a very credible organization had endorsed Akhuwat and he was therefore completely satisfied.

Case 404548 got a loan for his wife who was a master tailor. She once taught the skill for an NGO. They used the loan to get materials to make and repair clothes for men and women.

Case 502284 said her husband deserted her and she was raising two kids on her own. She bought a stitching machine with her loan. She said she used to do hand embroidery and spent eight to nine days before on one suit for which she charged Rs. 800. With the machine she was able to makes two suits in one day and charged Rs. 150 per suit. She said her business was doing well and she was thankful to Akhuwat since she would never commit the sin of taking a loan on interest. The organization has saved her from having to opt for a demeaning marriage to support her children.

Case 086567 took a loan for Rs. 25,000 and subsequently earned about Rs. 500 per day. He said, "I stopped taking loans because I feel like my needs are met and others should get them." He liked the groups because being in a group enabled them to help each other and institute *bhaichara*.

Case 731996 said he was a Christian and initially thought he would not get a loan for this reason. He discovered that with this organization there was no such bias. He said "their aim truly is to give and help those who are in need. It is like they hold your finger and walk along with you." He said, "The organization is good – if you cooperate with them they cooperate with you."

We explained in Chapter 6 that we did not use ten filled-in questionnaires for the data analysis for various reasons. Nonetheless, case 0472 is interesting and so we included it. He had a motorcycle spare parts shop and used two loans to extend his business and also bought clothes from a large industrial city to sell locally for a profit. He planned to take more and said even though the loans size is small it is better than not getting any. He said if the loan size was bigger he would have used some of the funds to buy a cow to sell milk as well. However, thanks to the loans his wife and son are also gainfully employed.

Summary

Our findings suggest that the organization has so far been successful in attaining its mission of promoting self-enterprise. Nine-tenths of respondents reported a substantial increase in household income due to the loan, and four-fifths reported that they paid back their loans exclusively from their earnings. Seventy percent of the borrowers were able to pay back on time. Eighty-five percent said they fully attained the business objective they set out to accomplish, and another 13 percent said this was somewhat the case. Only 2 percent reported they failed in their objective, and the reason cited was the lack of a market. While an overwhelming percentage of borrowers expressed satisfaction with what they had accomplished and were very positive about the organization, about half thought that the loan size needed to be larger.

Akhuwat has a very flexible and pragmatic approach to lending. We discovered an interesting example of this in villages and small towns located near Sialkot City, the center of one of Pakistan's premier exporting hubs. Factory owners like to pass on their overheads by sub-contracting tasks to home-based workers. Given rising energy costs, some home-based workers were balking at this business practice. Some workers were finding it more profitable to buy their own equipment and rent a factory space. Akhuwat facilitated this ownership of capital by workers which enhanced their leverage relative to factory owners.

Some of the externalities or macro impacts that Akhuwat had in its areas of operation include driving interest-based micro-credit out of the market. Akhuwat encourages this and is even willing to help borrowers with a loan (liberation loan) if they have only a few installments left to pay of an interest-based loan. It has been deaf to the bitter complaints of interest-based microcredit-NGOs who often move to another locality.

Akhuwat helps the labor market with the extensive on-the-job training it provides its staff at the training academy set up in Lahore City. The skills and work ethic instilled in the staff serve other organizations well as junior staff move on.

Akhuwat also has a salutary impact on the product market. Scholars studying microcredit (see Chapter 4) have noted the "fallacy of composition" such that what works for say one vendor may not work for scores. Perhaps Akhuwat minimizes this impact with its careful review of business plans.

In any case, since only 2 percent of borrowers noted the lack of a market as contributing to their inability to attain their objective, there is no evidence to support the fallacy of composition hypothesis in Akhuwat's case so far.

The case studies mostly reinforce the survey findings and self-sufficiency is a recurring theme in the narratives. Providing funds to enable workers to acquire machinery or supplies appears to be the way Akhuwat attains its stated mission of "alleviating poverty by empowering socially and economically marginalized families through interest free microfinance and by harnessing entrepreneurial potential, capacity building and social guidance." While a few respondents expressed their frustration with issues like collective group responsibility and rude field staff behavior pertaining to late payments, the majority of the respondents who shared their stories with us were positive about the organization and their loan experience. Many felt that their business was blessed and had succeeded because a loan from this organization was blessed.

Akhuwat's premise that loans are a household rather than an individual affair appears to have been borne out by the many respondents we talked to. Some of their stories have been summarized in the case studies, and we found the households pitching together in a common endeavor. Sometimes parents took loans for offspring and vice versa and at other times husbands for wives or vice versa depending on whose documentation and identification papers were in order.

The group method of giving loans sometimes created accidental entrepreneurship when someone in the neighborhood joined the group to help others and then succeeded in a business undertaking they would not have otherwise engaged in. While the individualists viewed the group to be an unnecessary transactions cost, others found in the group a mechanism to reduce transactions cost such as by taking turns in making payments. Some were frustrated at having their loans tied to others via group loans and they would have preferred to be responsible solely for themselves rather than having their record jeopardized by someone else's poor performance. Others however liked having the mutual group support and often referred to Akhuwat's social philosophy of empathy and solidarity in this regard.

Appendix 7.1
Problems with designing an impact assessment study of Akhuwat's effectiveness

One could in principle design an impact assessment of Akhuwat loan effectiveness, but in our view there would be several problems with the design. First, loan effectiveness in impact assessment studies is usually defined as the extent to which the micro-loan enhances the borrower's income. Since Akhuwat's mission is to engender social solidarity and self-reliance, measuring income enhancement would not be doing justice to what the organization is about. Second, individuals select themselves into borrower status when their community solicits Akhuwat's services. Third, individuals select themselves into the loan program by applying for the loans. Fourth, they are selected by Akhuwat based on stringent criteria (Akhuwat's social and business plan appraisals).

Suppose we do manage to find a likely community that is similar in all respects to one that is being served by Akhuwat but that has not yet solicited an Akhuwat program. We would then have to identify a group that is likely to apply for Akhuwat loans. After that, we would need to solicit Akhuwat's help in identifying who the likely candidates for the loan are. But this is unethical since individuals would not be granted a loan but would simply serve the study's purpose of identifying a control group.

Suppose instead that the researchers have the capacity to apply the criteria as Akhuwat would have done, which is unlikely, we finally arrive at a control. We would then have a benchmark and compare earnings of the control group and the treatment group in another community that actually received Akhuwat loans.

Our contention is that points one to four above suggests that selection is part of the design and therefore not an empirical issue that needs to be dealt with as is the case with conventional microcredit. However, even if selection bias was an issue that did need to be dealt with, the researcher's ability to identify a reasonable control group would be limited as explained above.

Ignoring the selection by design issue, suppose for the moment that it is possible to identify a reasonable control group. Many of the loans that

Akhuwat makes are to enable borrows to revive and enable the flourishing of an ongoing business. It would therefore be very difficult to econometrically parse the contribution of the initiative, energy, entrepreneurial talent and effort of borrowers from that of the loan. Using labor as an input in the production function (ignoring the other theoretical problems of using this tool) would not do this heterogeneous contribution justice. Similarly the capital input ratio of borrowers and the organization would be a very poor way of sorting out the capital contribution.

So far, we have not mentioned the conventional reason to be skeptical of reported numbers that impact assessments would need to be based on. None of the small entrepreneurs we interviewed kept records and their reported profits were guesstimates. We stopped asking these questions after a while and avoided reporting the numbers we did collect in the text.

For various reasons mentioned in the Preface, we have little faith in randomized control trials (RCT) being used in the social sciences. Based on the arguments proffered above, we have even less reason to believe that an RCT would be a useful exercise in evaluating Akhuwat's success in creating self-enterprise.

Notes

1 However, it negates this competitive ethic in its organizational philosophy by being willing to forego organizational sustainability in the conventional microfinance sense. The pairing of new business owners with older ones for mentorship and its message of empathy and solidarity also indicates more nuance beyond transmitting purely self-seeking and competitive values.
2 For more details on the Akhuwat microcredit model refer to Chapter 5.
3 We selected to limit repetition since many business narratives were similar.
4 We did not attempt an impact assessment and do not believe one is possible. Refer to Appendix 7.1 for our reasoning. We could have used data collected by the organization on its business appraisal forms (Appendix 6.7), but here the same reporting bias that we confronted in the field is likely and also data collected by the organization could be considered biased by readers.
5 Mason (2015, p. 186–87) cites scholarship suggesting that some Canadian workers in the 19th century owned their own tools and the term for a strike was "taking their tools out of the shop."
6 The AKRSP is one of Pakistan's first and most prominent development NGOs. Refer to Khan and Khan (1992) for a supportive account.
7 The case numbers are fictitious and created to preserve respondent anonymity but simultaneously to enable us to identify their quantitative and qualitative information if necessary for follow-up analysis.
8 Committee is the local term for a ROSCA (Rotating Saving and Credit Association). Refer to Appendix 6.8 for a comparison of a ROSCA to an Akhuwat loan.
9 The issues of group loans and co-signing have been discussed in Chapter 6, and we note comments pertaining to this issue in the case narratives if there is a novel perspective.

134 *Empirical assessment*

10 Praise for the organization was near universal. Since this is captured in Chapter 6, to avoid repetition we omitted these comments going forward. Negative comments were rare so we included most such comments.
11 Akhuwat had a guarantor method in place for approving loans but now prefers giving group loan.
12 We came across another unhappy borrower but are including his complaints in an endnote since he said little about his business. Case 76243 said he had been taking loans for between two and three years for butter manufacturing. He accused one field staff member of asking for the installment early and also of being a drug addict. He accused another of taking the installment without recording it and hence made him a defaulter. He said he had to say nice things about the field staff when he had a loan outstanding but since he was no longer a borrower, he was not obligated and could tell the truth. He conceded that the loan had enabled him to shift from being a laborer to being self-sufficient. However, he needed another loan but they were unjustly denying him. He said they only gave loans to their friends or used them for their own purposes. He even accused them of recording a donation on his receipt to look good when he had not made one. The latter accusation did not make sense because recording a donation without receiving one would mean that the unit managers would be liable to cover the amount on the receipt out of pocket. The former accusations about the field officers were an outlier given how positively all the other borrowers spoke of them. It seems that even Akhuwat cannot please everyone.
13 Muslim celebratory holy day.
14 Clearly he understood Marx's concept of surplus value and exploitation.
15 Perhaps he meant that Akhuwat subsequently invests the pooled resources for a fixed return. We discuss Akhuwat's accounts in Chapter 8.

References

Khan, M. H. and S. Sultan Khan. 1992. *Rural Change in the Third World: Pakistan and the Aga Khan Rural Support Program* (New York: Greenwood Press).

Mason, P. 2015. Post Capitalism: A Guide to Our Future (New York: Farrar, Straus and Giroux).

Udovitch, A. L. 1970. *Partnership and Profit in Medieval Islam* (Princeton: Princeton University Press).

8 Policy issues

Introduction

While much of what is contained in this chapter is directed to Akhuwat, the issues discussed have salience for other microcredit organizations. We discuss a number of issues starting with how the organization both conformed to but also defied and changed the local culture. We next discuss a number of issues that we flagged when discussing survey findings in Chapters 6 and 7. In particular we discuss group loans but also take up the tricky issue of the organization's need to be both inclusive and exclusive at the same time in its loan provision. We discuss the name of the organization and how that embodies the vision it propagates but how the reality of managing a successful loan program and taking that to scale could be challenged by that vision. Similarly, there are seeming ideological inconsistencies in the very nature of the lending it is engaged in on the asset and liability side. In this context we discuss the concepts of *riba* and interest, organizational accounts and sustainability. We discuss the core strengths of the organization such as its field staff dedication and policy coherence and revisit the issue of the method of donation collection. We end with suggestions for the organization from the field.

Defying local culture

The organization is widely perceived as having deep religious roots and strong cultural support since it is engaged in eliminating the curse of interest consistent with Islamic teaching. Perhaps the self-confidence that comes from this, but certainly Dr. Saqib's progressive beliefs, enables the organization to defy local culture in ways other NGOs may be reluctant to.

There sometimes was resentment in the field that the staff did not even accept water in very hot temperatures contrary to cultural practices of the extension and acceptance of hospitality. However, there was also a great deal of admiration for this Spartan policy and many appreciate that the purpose was to emphasize the point that "they are only here to serve and not to take." Also the organization did not want to impose any burden on the very poorest who might feel compelled to serve tea and clearly this saved staff time. Even cold water can be a burden on the poor who do not have refrigerators and would have to borrow from friends or neighbors. Thus despite the extreme heat, the staff refrained from accepting water.

Requiring spouses to accompany beneficiaries to the office to sign off on loans serves the purposes of informing the household that loans are being taken to avoid abuse of loans by one household member without knowledge of the others. A mutual warranty ensures mutual responsibility, and it is also critical for the financial sustainability of the revolving fund used to give loans since household members serve as warrantee for each other and this facilitates loan collection.

While the majority of the borrowers approved co-signing loans (70 percent of the women and 57 percent of the men), the requirement that both co-signers be present in the mosque during the loan distribution ceremony created some resentment. Many male respondents viewed it as violating cultural norms of *purdah* (screening women from male strangers). While in principle one may welcome the encouragement of women's mobility in a very culturally conservative context and also their access to public spaces like mosques, women often resented this policy even more since it represented income foregone for the men who had to accompany them.[1] Some women mentioned they were mortified and guilt ridden that they had to attend a check distribution function in a mosque when menstruating.

Many argued that when the organization staff visits the home for the first investigation, all in the household are made aware of the loan. That they feel is a good time to secure signatures if necessary and that further requirements of co-signatures are an unnecessary transaction cost imposed on family members. The check distribution ceremony however is very important for the organization in reinforcing its teaching regarding other consciousness and social solidarity. These complaints notwithstanding, 85 percent rated the organizational procedures as very good and 8 percent as good.

Other examples of defying local culture are Akhuwat's work on behalf of the transgender community despite the cultural stigma attached to this community. An inclusive cross-faith hiring policy and promoting members of other faiths like Christianity to senior managerial positions and celebrating Christmas for Christian staff is another example. The bias against Christian staff members in the general public is reflected in the following comment we received during fieldwork: "I rated the organization 4 instead of 5 (five being the best) because the Branch Manager is Christian." He nevertheless mentioned that nobody else does such good work.

Organizational vs. social needs

Group loans

The organization needs groups as a mechanism for social pressure for loan recoveries although it also claims that group solidarity embodies Akhuwat or *bhaichara* (brotherhood) and hence the use of groups. Group members are expected to help each other in repayments if necessary and keep each other on track. But many in focus group discussions (FGDs) told us that the poorest find it difficult to be included. Similarly, the organization is more comfortable lending to homeowners (at least one in the group needs to be a homeowner) since they are less transient and an anchor to trace other group members if needed, which raises the odds of getting a loan for the relatively more prosperous.[2]

Loan size

Many reported the amount they received was too small relative to their needs (44 percent). One businessman argued that he employed three helpers and could have hired more with more support. The organizational need is to start small, partly due to funding constraints and partly because that enables them to monitor the case record to weed out potential defaulters. While it has been very rare, some borrowers try to game the system by establishing a good case record (timely payments) to get a larger loan and then become tardy.

While the organization tries to monitor closely (83 percent of the loans monitored), it is difficult to do this for ongoing businesses since money is fungible and inventories could have been bought with other funds. Thus the misuse of funds is possible. This was of particular concern in one branch where the area office preferred individual loans since they feared loan "hijacking." This was described as a group pooling funds to turn over to one user because the loan size was small. The user then took responsibility to pay back for the remaining group members. In this regard, it is entirely possible for one person in the group to be motivated to have others sign on because of his/her need and for the rest to use the funds partly for consumption purposes.

Intra-group conflict

There may also be a conflict in the needs of group members. Some would like to pay off the loan quickly so they can qualify for a larger repeat loan. The organization however has extended the repayment period and reduced installment size to ease the burden on the poorest. Some members pointed out that they understand why this was done but that nonetheless this did not serve their need. In one case a member complained that she did not get a repeat loan because she paid off the loan early hence inadvertently signaling that she was not really needy and therefore not a good candidate for a loan.

Inclusivity vs. selectivity

Inclusivity is part of the organization's social philosophy, and yet it needs to be highly selective when giving loans to protect its ability to continue to lend. While the social appraisal identifies if the potential borrower is truly poor and thus in need of organizational support, they also explore credit risk by talking to neighbors. It is clear that, at least for now, only the poor deemed responsible or good credit risks can be assisted.

The selectivity also excludes the very elderly, and one fit elderly person claimed this to be "ageism." He argued that he was as capable as his sons to use the loans well if not more so, and that excluding him because he was elderly was not fair.[3] Others complained about the exclusion of single men based on the policy of giving loans to households. A Christian man was puzzled by the rule that they had to have a Muslim in their group. While this could promote interfaith harmony, it placed the burden on Christians to find a Muslim to join their group.

Operational issues

Bhaichara vs. hierarchy

The organization has to maintain a delicate balance between the need for hierarchy for efficiency and yet have staff internalize the egalitarian message of *bhaichara* (brotherhood). Organizational efficiency can require a hierarchical structure such as the one Akhuwat uses with well-defined positions for regional, area, branch and unit managers/loan officers with assistant positions at each level prior to full promotion to the higher level.

One could conceive of such hierarchy, which clearly exists also in terms of deference to seniors across the board, as contradicting Akhuwat's egalitarian message. However, several mechanisms are instituted as a countervailing force to hierarchy. All sitting around a table on cushions on the floor in the branch office and collectively cleaning the office prior to its opening is meant to be evocative of the spirit of Akhuwat.[4] One branch manager said he organizes social events with the unit managers to create camaraderie. While reporting is via proper channels, complete access and open lines of communications with seniors is also said to help.

Policy issues 139

Using religious spaces

This is important in Pakistan's context as civil society has become increasingly polarized in the post-9/11 bombings context. Initiatives to reclaim and potentially restore the mosques for general and pluralistic community purposes, as opposed to the default option of relinquishing spaces and allowing them to become hubs of extremist thought, are crucial and ought to be encouraged. A culture of actively holding institutions accountable at the community level, particularly in terms of inclusivity, has the potential to revive critical engagement which is constructive for social reconciliation. Akhuwat may not be deliberately addressing this social need, but it has enormous potential to do so, and consciousness of this role might be something for them to consider.

Monitoring

There is close monitoring of business loans. As earlier stated, 83 percent of respondents of business loans indicated that there was a unit manager visit after the loan had been sanctioned to make sure that the funds were utilized for the purpose intended. In practice this may be impossible to do (see explanation above). For example, there was one case of three friends who went in for a group loan, or Rs. 20,000 each. They then split the loan two ways contrary to official policy. However the loans were very successful. A rickshaw and potato chip vending yielded about Rs. 600 and Rs. 1,000 respectively daily, and they were comfortably able to pay back the loan. Despite this success, loan usage was against Akhuwat's stated policy and suggested a monitoring oversight. The worst-case scenario of course is individuals using loans to lend to others against agreed terms, but in close knit communities that Akhuwat works in such misuse of loan funds may be difficult to conceal.

As indicated earlier, in one branch such practices were referred to as "loan hi-jacking." The concern that this was happening caused branch offices to prefer individual loans. This also is difficult since the borrower needs two guarantors who have nothing to gain from the loan other than goodwill, and some even asked to be compensated for the time/transaction costs they incur as a result of the loan they endorsed (e.g. going to the office for signing papers).

Field staff

As indicated in Chapter 6, the most overwhelming view all across the country, with only a few exceptions, was about the excellent behavior of

140 *Empirical assessment*

the staff. The field cadre and sound policy are the foundation this organization is built on. At current salaries, many junior staff are willing to dedicate only a limited amount of time to serving in the organization even though they feel working for it represents a win-win – getting a salary to do good work.[5]

Ultimately, family compulsions prevail, and in their words the food allowance of Rs. 1,400 put into place to back up the policy of no local hires, to prevent nepotistic pressures, is meager. Many staff members commute to work from home towns many kilometers away and often on their own motor bikes. The staff can claim field expenses of Rs. 5 per case per month, so carrying an average of 100 cases would mean Rs. 500 per month and this could partly defray fuel costs for those choosing to own a motorbike. In addition they log in private bike mileage for official duty on the honor system and get reimbursed. Akhuwat staff is entitled to a provident fund, and the 10 percent deduction from basic salary is matched by an equal contribution from the organization (Finance and Accounts Manual).

Even so, the remuneration package is not competitive, and the loss of experienced field staff members is a loss of institutional knowledge.[6] Though systems are in place for staff hand overs in the form of registers and member contacts, there is nonetheless a loss and high turnover rates can undermine the strength of the organization. It is however a buyer's market with a surplus of young educated candidates looking for jobs, and so there is no shortage of replacements for junior staff.

The policy of using non-locals in branch offices and regular transfers of field staff can represent a loss of a link to the community and in community building. However, this policy also avoids nepotism whereby loans are extended to community members based on good relations with field staff. It minimizes pressure from family and friends on the field staff insisting on ethical behavior. Finally, it minimizes the appropriation of loans for own use by using community members as fronts. The organization clearly values the reality and perception of being completely fair and above board in loan distribution much more and hence is willing to accept this trade-off suggested above. However, one issue Akhuwat needs to consider carefully is the impact of their transfer policy on female staff. We sensed that female staff members are under pressure, often from their parents, to quit their jobs with Akhuwat because of their transfer policy.

The leadership's view is that staff are engaged in good work and not doing it for temporal benefits. Only those with a crusading and voluntarist spirit who have internalized Akhuwat's social philosophy of empathy and social solidarity are likely to stay on and build their careers within the organization. Promotion is from within the organization so those who are judged to identify with the organization's vision and mission, work hard, are perceived to be honest and effective (generate cases – borrowers) and have the necessary knowledge and experience move up the hierarchy.

The executive director estimated that staff put in about 10 to 15 hours overtime. The overtime is recorded at the branch level but not entered into the central management information system (MIS) for explicit use for promotions. The executive director viewed overtime as a signal that a staff member has internalized the organizational vision of dedicated service which is among the criteria used for promotion. Ultimately, it is difficult to distinguish working for promotion from selfless dedication. However, either way, the demonstrated or actual dedication eases the 'principal-agent' problem and field-staff deliver on head office objectives. There could be a negative aspect to staff donations and overtime since demonstrating dedication might amount to self-exploitation at best and organizational exploitation at worst.

Pragmatism and policy changes

Policy changes occur as the organization evolves to address issues of equity and efficiency and they are generally applied uniformly across the board.[7] They are often thoughtful and designed to address issues arising from the field. In fact, we found that pragmatism and innovation are the norm with Akhuwat. For example, early reports suggested a flat management structure given the high level of volunteerism among senior staff. Our visits and fieldwork (2015) showed that its organization structure of necessity had become hierarchical particularly at the field level, though camaraderie at all levels was still readily discernible.

The 5 percent loan membership fee introduced to ensure the funds were valued, as a "free lunch" might not, was discontinued, and our findings showed the loans were nonetheless highly valued. Initially it was thought that having field-staff serve their own community would facilitate outreach and recovery, but this policy was subsequently changed to avoid nepotism and pressure on the field staff from family, friends and acquaintances. Many of our respondents appreciated the lack of favoritism and nepotism in the decision making process.

Initially field staff helped with group formation, and the group leaders had considerable autonomy and could abuse their position. Women formed self-help groups of about ten women (as with Indian microfinance – see Chapter 4) and saving Rs. 3,000 was mandatory before loans were issued. This practice was phased out in favor of individual loans with two guarantors. However, many had difficulties in finding guarantors and others avoided being guarantors because they thought they would be liable. The policy of loans to guarantors depending on the borrower paying back the loan created an incentive for peer pressure and was discontinued. This however meant that guarantors in the community had no skin in the game but were simply expected to be good Samaritans. The reality was that many felt they should be compensated for the income foregone for the time spent and for the transactions cost incurred.

By the time we did our field work, Akhuwat had moved back to groups of between three and six and individuals formed their own groups. However, the initiative for installment collection was with the unit managers rather than the group head as earlier. The guarantor option remained for those not able to be included in a group and some branches still preferred this option more generally.

There are clearly advantages of having smaller self-selected groups when they work well and they are a vehicle for Akhuwat's efforts of creating social solidarity. Group members often help each other out even to the extent of helping each other with installments. Allowing any one member of a group to submit installments on behalf of the others reduces transactions costs for others in the group. Allowing flexibility in group size can reduce transactions cost. The minimum size is three, but having more means that even if a group member drops out the group remains intact.

However, problems remain as indicated in Chapter 6, and so more policy changes are likely. About half the respondents, while mostly feeling positive about their group experience, said they would prefer individual loans. Often individuals of very different capacities need to work together. Some wanted to pay off loans quickly to qualify for another loan. Some resented their record being tarnished by others who were tardy and the transaction costs and the peer pressure and discord could undermine social capital. To assist the poorest the organization extended the repayment period and reduced the size of the installment. All group members notwithstanding the heterogeneity were bound by this policy change, and, while many were deeply appreciative, others resented the delay this meant is their efforts to secure another loan.

Some reservations and ideological inconsistencies

Akhuwat's partners and role of religion: social justice versus morality

Dr. Amjad Saqib's message, completely internalized by most of the field staff, is that what counts is the goodness of a person and the organization is blind to all else (religion, gender, ethnicity). There is every indication that this message is implemented by the field staff. Yet the organization's partners are the local religious influentials who deliver the keynote addresses during loan distribution ceremonies, and we saw this message reinforced and supplemented by an area manager much in the same style as Friday sermons are delivered. In fact, some refer to Akhuwat as the *maulvi* (Muslim preacher) bank. Since the vision of *maulvis* is often much narrower than that of the organization they serve, providing the former with so much credibility can be problematic to those who espouse a more progressive vision of Islam. Similarly, Akhuwat's engagement with the transgender community is interesting and a case-study on the question of gender engagement within a religious framework. Deriving values through religion may be more broadly accepted if they are premised on social justice rather than moralistic constructs of respectability.

The name

Akhuwat means *bhaichara* or brotherhood. While the concept refers to social solidarity that is inclusive of women, the term *bhaichara* semantically excludes them. In fact, this is not something that the organization intends since the loans are to the households and 42 percent of the loans in our sample were received by women. Akhuwat is now a functioning and very successful brand name and the name is unlikely to be changed but its literature could focus more on the social solidarity and empathy aspect of the concept rather than the brotherhood aspect.

Riba and interest

Following Haque (1995), we adopt the broader definition of *riba* as social exploitation when fixed predetermined value is appropriated without giving in return social value in the form of assuming risk or human effort that creates value. Further, *riba* emerges in this definition when there is uneven power in a contract or exchange between parties (see discussion in Khan, 1987, Chapter 1). Based on this broader definition, the interest charged by banks, rents charged by landlords, or monopoly rents can all be construed to represent an appropriation of value that constitutes *riba* in so far as they are based on unequal power between parties to the contracts or exchange. Similarly the extraction of surplus value in the Marxian framework based on an unequal power relationship between capital and labor (or due to imperfect markets in the neo-classical framework) could be viewed as *riba*.

In all cases, value is appropriated without giving equivalent counter value and there is uneven power involved in the exchange or contract. This broader definition suggests that for *riba* to be absent from a contract or exchange, both conditions have to be met. The narrow definition assumed by most contemporary scholars and practitioners merely equates *riba* with all forms of interest, received or taken, and this is the definition adopted by Akhuwat.

Based on the broader definition or *riba* that we adopt, interest charged to the very poorest by microfinance institutions is a form of social exploitation. This is the case because the microfinance loan in and of itself does not constitute adequate counter value since risk or human effort (labor creating value) is not provided in exchange. Also, there is an uneven power relationship between the microfinance institution and its clients.

However, using this broader definition, the interest received from banks per se is not social exploitation if it does not entail the taking of value based on an uneven power relationship. However, if the real rate of interest is positive, there is still the taking of value without giving equivalent counter value and hence such taking of positive real rate of interest constitutes *riba*.

As stated earlier, Akhuwat accepts the narrow definition of *riba* as the giving and taking of all interest. We informed them that this creates an organizational inconsistency since they accept a pre-announced fixed return on their investments. The chief financial officer informed us that the returns they get on their long term deposits are declared to be sharia (Islamic Law) compliant, i.e. they are invested in a sharia consistent manner and they are only informed of an expected rate of return and not a specific positive rate. Furthermore, sometimes the actual return falls below or above the pre-announced range. Even so, Akhuwat's Finance and Accounts Manual acknowledges bank deposits (short-term), purchase of bonds, debt securities and debentures as possible investments and all of these represent fixed income.

Initially Akhuwat's stated policy was to nurture their borrowers so that they could graduate and move on to the conventional banking system for further business loans.[8] But this violates Akhuwat's ideological opposition to interest. Again, pragmatism rules and we support it. There is no getting around the fact that Akhuwat operates in an interest-based economic environment and is likely to do so for the foreseeable future.

Charity is visible and for some not voluntary[9]

Only a few respondents actually verbalized their suspicion that the voluntary contributions represented an implicit interest rate. We calculated borrower donations in 2015 to be 0.001 percent of total operating income. This amount is so small that we think the organization should experiment with anonymous mechanisms of collecting contributions to avoid jeopardizing the immense goodwill among borrowers that it has painstakingly built. We have proposed a study to evaluate a transition as Appendix 8.1 since this issue is central to our concern with altruism in this book.

The goodwill for Akhuwat is so immense that many even defended the current method of donation collection. One respondent challenged the claim that it was interest by pointing out that "the donations were not fixed and pre-specified." In the spirit of social solidarity, Akhuwat believes that those who take must give to help others and many indeed indicated that to be their reason for giving. However, many viewed the recording of donations and making this public as violating religious norms since in Islam it is preferable that charitable contributions be anonymous. One respondent said, "They ask every month: it is not like you can avoid giving."

In Chapter 2 we put forward a working definition of altruism as occurring when people contribute to the material well-being of others without any guarantee of a material reward for themselves as a consequence, direct or indirect, of that contribution. The emphasis is on the word material as well as on the lack of causal consequence between the act of giving and any guaranteed future material gain. With public giving and receipts issued, individuals could be motivated by their desire for repeat loans. Similarly, while staff contributions are not recorded at the individual level, once again, these donations are not pure altruism since there could be implicit managerial coercion.

Moral pressure

Public funding raises another concern. Given that 99 percent of its credit pool currently is public money, Akhuwat is effectively imposing social values with public money. Many are values that are laudable, but in a democracy the use of public money to impose values is not acceptable. For example, not giving loans to a tobacco shop because intoxication is haram (religiously prohibited) is acceptable if a financial NGO is using private money but questionable if it is doing so with public money unless backed by legislation.

Accounts and sustainability

Harper[10] suggested that Akhuwat has turned the traditional concept of sustainability on its head and, rather than focus on the sustainability of the organization, it focuses on the sustainability of the household. Even so, it can engage in good works as long as it is around, and there is little indication that Akhuwat is intending to phase out by exhausting the credit pool it is painstakingly building. In fact Akhuwat is very conservative with the use of its funds and runs an operating surplus, and 44 percent of borrowers thought that its loan size should be bigger.

Akhuwat is expanding rapidly (Appendix 5.1).[11] Based on its Audit Report for the year ended June 30, 2016,[12] its main source of operating income was derived from operating fees from funds forwarded to it from various mostly government agencies. It had a credit pool of Rs. 5.6 billion (99 percent of total liabilities) with Rs. 5 billion of it from the Punjab Small Industries Corporation. It was entitled to a 7 percent service fee on the disbursed amount for its operational needs. Most economists would consider this an incentive to push disbursements. Yet Akhuwat remains conservative notwithstanding the high demand and pressure from borrowers for larger loan sizes (Chapters 6 and 7).

The other much smaller but notable contributions to its credit pool were from the Government of Gilgit and Baltistan (Rs. 210 million for five years starting April 15, 2013) and from Pakistan Poverty Alleviation Fund under the Prime Minister's Interest Free Loan Scheme (Rs. 336 million for four years starting April 12, 2014, with a 10 percent service charge).[13] Loans from individuals (7 percent) need to pick up or Akhuwat will be reliant on the goodwill of particular administrations.[14]

The immense goodwill it has amassed at the grassroots level could be leveraged into voluntary contributions as its current and ex-borrower size increases.[15] Akhuwat hopes that its good work will get known by word of mouth and it will solicit donations from the broader community much as Edhi Foundation (Pakistan's most well-known charitable foundation, http://edhi.org/) has, and ultimately this might be the path to its financial sustainability. Its donated fund represented 15 percent of total assets so it has received generous contributions from well-wishers and supporters.

Apart from regular fund-raising events, opening a deposit bank is another mechanism for financial sustainability that Akhuwat is pursuing. According to the executive director, deposits will be interest free and only a current account service would be provided. About half the funds will be invested in *sharia* (Islamic Law) compliant investments to cover operations. The remaining half will be used for its *Qarz-e-Hassn* (interest-free) loans. The executive director pointed out that many wanted to park their funds with such a deposit bank for a few years but were not in a position to give a grant. This bank will provide them with an avenue to contribute in the future with their deposits.[16]

Suggestions from the field

We solicited open ended suggestions from borrowers for the organization. The largest number (110) simply expressed good wishes for the organization and prayed that it continue and enhance its good work on behalf of the poor. We have constructed Appendix 8.2 by coding the responses since they made multiple suggestions. We interpret these responses as indicative of the strength of their feelings.

For example, while slightly over half said they preferred an individual to a group loan, only 21 individuals mentioned it as a recommendation for procedural change to the organization. Similarly, while a fifth of female and 28 percent of male borrowers opposed loan co-signing, once again only four individuals bought it up as a suggestion for procedural change. Again while 43 percent did not approve of receiving borrower donations publicly to a direct question, only five suggested anonymous donations as a procedural change. One however felt very strongly that donations should not be announced in the mosque since this carries the lack of anonymity to a higher level.

Fifty-six percent thought the business loan size was too small, and 66 (second largest frequency) suggested enhancing the loan size as a recommendation. Six individuals suggested that Akhuwat ensure that its field-staff improve their behavior towards borrowers. Since this represents 2 percent of our total sample, Akhuwat does not have a big problem on its hands in this regard.

There were some other interesting suggestions that came during conversations and discussions that we recorded. One suggested that Akhuwat should institute a medical emergency loan. Akhuwat could partner with hospitals and directly pay the bills, and the beneficiaries could then pay back Akhuwat. Three borrowers suggested that Akhuwat should enable borrowers to transfer funds via mobile accounts. Not having to go personally would save on transactions cost.

Group members in a FGD in Islamabad indicated that the transactions cost of getting loans were very high. One suggestion to reduce them was separating application from installment collection timings to reduce the size of the queue. Another suggestion was having a field staff member post collection times at a community mosque for collection once a month. This could save many borrowers much time and transport cost of coming to the branch office for making payments.

In the male FGD, men spoke against the practice of female members in their household having to go in public to co-sign a loan in a mosque. This is particularly so since everyone in the household already knows of the loan so requiring their co-signing is redundant. However, only two brought this up as suggestions for procedural change.[17]

Another suggestion during a FGD was that if the loan is not granted, the fee should be re-funded since the organization does not incur the expense of administering the loan. We did not point out that the administrative expense had already been incurred, but the field-staff might point this out. In one FGD a social explanation was provided for why the loan size should be larger. They argued that this would create more livelihoods as people would have the ability hire others when operating on a larger scale.

Summary

As indicated in earlier chapters, we believe that overall Akhuwat is delivering on its vision and mission statement of creating social solidarity and self-sufficiency respectively. We discovered a number of tensions during the fieldwork suggesting that Akhuwat often has to walk a fine line to do so. Even its name embodies a tension. While the meaning of Akhuwat (*bhaichara* or brotherhood) is a noble concept, it excludes half the population. In practice, it clearly does not do that.

The organization has secured enormous goodwill from abolishing interest-based transactions and uses that to slowly bring about progressive cultural change such as encouraging access to women in public spaces, more say for them in handling credit and the household economy, and promoting interfaith harmony. Christians are encouraged to partner with Muslims in group formation and welcomed to mosques for loan distribution ceremonies. This progressive vision could be challenged by its use of mosque functionaries as partners. Since it is identified with the abolition of interest, it is possible that fundamentalists with a much narrower vision may seek to join this endeavor.

Group formation is where the organizational need for using social pressure for loan recovery is most at odds with borrower's preferences. Groups are entirely consistent with the organizational philosophy to inculcate social solidarity. There were certainly examples of group members helping each other. Yet we heard of many cases of conflict within the groups when some were tardy and hence spoiled the record (being marked a defaulter in the extreme case) of others in the group and undermined others ability to secure a repeat loan. While the intent is building social solidarity, the effect may be that of undermining it. Only 30 percent expressed a preference for group loans.

Similar tensions exist operationally. The organization seeks to alleviate and indeed eradicate poverty. Yet, it needs to preserve its revolving fund and be as effective as possible in recovering loans and granting new ones. Hence, it needs to select borrowers carefully, vet them and monitor in order to recover its loans. Exclusion to some extent is inevitable due to the funding constraint the organization operates under.

Again, *bhaichara* (brotherhood or solidarity) could be thought of as an organizational motto and this suggests fraternity and egalitarianism. Yet organizational efficiency requires a hierarchy and once again the organization had pragmatically dealt with this. All the field staff sits on the floor and also jointly cleans the office and this promotes a spirit of equality and solidarity. Yet lines of authority and reporting are clearly defined.

While it places a heavy emphasis on trust and the honor system it has put systems in place to avoid nepotism and to ensure transparency. For example, field staff does not serve in their own community and are often transferred. Despite a remuneration package that is well below other comparator civil society organizations its annual turnover rates are modest.

We take issue with Akhuwat on two points. First it adopts a narrow definition of *riba* as merely all forms of interest rather than a broader definition that equates *riba* with the taking of value without giving in exchange equivalent counter value in terms of assuming risk of providing labor. Further, by this broader definition, *riba* is involved when the appropriation in a transaction is based on unequal power relations in a contract. Since we are not Islamic scholars, we can merely point this out. However, a perusal of Akhuwat's accounts suggests the use of debt instruments on the asset side which would be considered *riba* by the definition it has adopted.

Second, Akhuwat encourages altruistic donations among its borrowers as part of its vision of promoting social solidarity. Since Akhuwat collects donations publicly and issues a receipt in exchange, borrowers are being subjected to social pressure in this public method of collection. The motivations might be altruistic anyway, but they could also be driven by seeking good standing among the field staff to ensure a repeat loan. Similarly staff contributions appear to be subject to implicit managerial coercion and hence donations may not conform to pure altruism.

While Akhuwat has strong public support and its audit report ending June 30, 2016, showed donations amounted to 15 percent of its accumulated liabilities, the bulk of its liabilities represented a Credit Pool for making loans. The bulk of the funds came from large government donations. Five billion were from the Punjab Small Industries Corporation. One could quibble and argue that Akhuwat really promotes self-employment rather than small industries. But we are not inclined to quibble given the evidence we reviewed pertaining to its effectiveness in creating self-sufficiency according to its mission statement. However, relying to such a large extent on government programs can be risky.

There were many suggestions from the field by borrowers suggesting procedural change. The procedural change recommended with the second-largest frequency was enhancing the size of the loan. The suggestion that occurred with the largest frequency was actually not about procedural change but simply that it would be impossible to improve upon what Akhuwat was already doing and therefore that they should do more of what they were already doing.

Appendix 8.1
Proposed RCT (randomized control trial) on voluntary giving

Introduction and background

Akhuwat wants to turn borrowers (members) into givers (donors) as one of the central aspects of its social philosophy. The key mechanisms it uses to achieve this purpose are *tabligh* (teaching or delivering a message) that draws on enlightened Islamic traditions in particular and humanitarianism in general. An operational mechanism currently utilized to achieve this goal is "voluntary" donations at the time of installment repayments. The donation is duly noted on a receipt along with the payment of an installment at the branch office.

The records of the donations make them auditable and provide assurance to the member donors in case some have doubts about misappropriation at the branch office level and also at the member group level, where one member is sometimes entrusted to submit installments and donations on behalf of the rest and a few members stated they feel reassured when receiving the receipt.

Our findings (Chapter 6) indicate that some members do not care about what happens to the funds they give. They give for Allah and that is enough. Receipts may not necessarily be important for them. Others appear to have internalized Akhuwat's social philosophy of empathy and give to help others just as they have been helped. We used the word "appear" because it is quite possible that this is a social philosophy they live by on their own but it must certainly have been reinforced by Akhuwat's teaching. For this set of people, receipts may be important as their reasons indicate interest in the use of funds being channeled right, as opposed to just blindly giving in the name of religion.

Finally, there are other responses that object to the current operational mechanism of recorded giving. They do so because in their view giving in Islam is preferable when anonymous, a norm violated by the current operational mechanism. Several suggested that such public giving is "for show." We noted that others gave because they felt coerced. Some indicated it was difficult to give a small amount because we were being observed and others thought that their next loan might be conditioned on if and how much they give. In some cases, members thought that "forced" donations were a form of implicit interest. In one case a member was ejected from the group for not giving enough because the remaining members thought this would tarnish their record.

These doubts occurred despite repeated assurance from the field staff that the giving was entirely voluntary. Even so, since the members felt subject to social pressure of how much other group members gave and the observations of the field staff, an element of perceived coercion is present. The preference of this set of people regarding receipts is that they should not include the amount of donation given, in addition to the returned installment.

We think that encouraging altruistic giving is a laudable goal but that it can only be considered self-motivated or induced altruism (based on teaching) if it is entirely without any pressure, real or perceived. It is clear that Akhuwat has earned a tremendous amount of goodwill based on the interest-free loans they give and the near universal kindness, graciousness and courtesy of its field staff (Chapter 6). It is also clear that Akhuwat does not view these donations as relevant to its operational sustainability as indicated by the Executive Director. Furthermore, as indicated above, on a macro level these donations amounted to only 0.001 percent of its operational income. Given this, Akhuwat could be jeopardizing some of the enormous goodwill it is building at the grassroots level by putting into place a mechanism that may be perceived as contradicting its message of voluntary giving in the spirit of social solidarity.

In view of this, we propose a randomized control trial (RCT) to inform Akhuwat of the possibility of positive policy changes consistent with its vision. As social scientists the information is of value to us because it would be informative of human behavior.

Proposed pilot study

We propose randomly selecting about 5 to 10 percent from the total list of branches. Ten percent is normally the sample sized proposed by sampling statisticians for representative results, although even 5 percent may yield low enough sampling errors. The selected branches would continue to report voluntary donations using the current regime and will serve as the control group (group C). Using paired sampling methodology, the following procedures would be instituted at the nearest two branches to the selected branches.

In one set of branches (group A – anonymous), a collection box system would be instituted (of the kind Akhuwat originally had) but at a secure point in Akhuwat's branch offices but not observable by the field staff. In the other set of branches (group B – both), members would be given a choice of using either the current regime or the group A regime which would also be instituted. The key to the boxes could be in the possession of a community member held in high trust based on the recommendation of the steering committee.

At the end of each month, borrowers could be invited to witness the public counting, and due procedures would be followed to enable auditing and ensure confidence and procedural credibility. One possibility is that the donation boxes be opened during the check distribution ceremony. Alternatively, this could be a separate and dedicated counting ceremony held in the mosque to which all current and past members are invited. This would be another follow-up opportunity to impart Akhuwat's teachings on social solidarity.

Our conjecture is that on the one hand, collections might decline if social pressure is inducing donations. However, this would be valuable information, and this could be offset by more nuanced teaching. On the other hand, we would know that those that give in group A (and some in Group B) branches do so out of a pure spirit of altruism. What drives that altruistic motive would not be straight forward to interpret – it could be motivated by reward in the hereafter or empathy that the organization attempts to culti-. vate – but Akhuwat's teaching clearly has an impact. Similarly, interpretation of the voluntary giving for branches in group B would not be straight forward.

These alternative operational mechanisms might be a way of inducing healthy branch level competition for both members and field staff to induce donations. However, what matters in the final analysis is that the donations be based on altruistic motives rather than any form of coercion. We suggest collecting data for the three set of branches (A, B and C) for a period of six months.

Hypothesis

The maintained hypothesis is that there will be lower collections in A relative to C as predicted by neo-classical postulates on maximizing behavior. If this is falsified, it could be due to the teachings on empathy and social solidarity instilled by the organization or because neo-classical postulates are not fully able to explain the complexity of human behavior or both. Even if humans respond to these particular teachings which are consistent with their faith, this would still justify a process of re-theorizing as suggested by Vernon Smith (Chapter 2) since the increase in giving would be consistent with our working definition of altruism (Chapter 2).

Appendix 8.2
Borrower suggestions for the organization

Suggestions	n
Should give bigger loans	66
It is not possible to make it any better	54
They should expand and help more people	56
Should provide option for choice between individual or group loan	21
They should provide an option for paying back installments individually	4
Loans should not be cosigned	4
Loans should be collected via anonymous donation boxes	5
Improve staff behavior	6
Be more selective in giving loans	8
Move to mobile banking	3
More flexibility regarding repayments	7
They should not function in mosques	3
Be quicker in processing loans	5
Should not indulge in nepotism	2
Should not require having a homeowner in the group	3
Find ways of reducing transactions costs	10
Should not distinguish between Christians and Muslims	2
Women should not have to go to the Mosque	2

Source: Author fieldwork

Notes: n = Total number making suggestions

Notes

1 In one case the check collection was not in a mosque but in a shrine and a woman complained this was very humiliating (*zilalat*) with so many men present. She felt that the mosque would have been much better.
2 In some small areas like Skardu, homeownership is not an issue since borrowers are easy to trace unlike in the bigger cities.
3 The exclusion may be based on the cultural expectation that children will take care of the elderly.
4 One table with cushions around it on the floor, a file cabinet or steel cupboard is not only evocative of the spirit of Akhuwat but keeps overheads low. This setting is similar to the sitting room areas in Skardu and Gamba in Gilgit-Baltistan

Policy issues 155

which the field staff considered very poor. In Punjab, a more prosperous Province, some sitting furniture is expected inside houses even if it is only *manjis* (rope beds).
5 It would be useful to compute labor turnover for the field staff and compare them to say the turnover rates for other civil society organizations in Pakistan. We were only able to get aggregate estimates of *annual* staff turnover rates of 7.4 percent for 2014 (staff that left / total staff *100, i.e. 116/1549*100). The Rural Support Program Network did not respond to our request for estimates but US rates can be used as a rough benchmark. In 2006, average turnover rates in the United States varied between around 15 percent annually for durable goods manufacturing employees to as high as 56 percent for the restaurant and hospitality industry (http://smallbusiness.chron.com/definition-high-turn over-rate-11272.html). Thus, rates vary a great deal so it is difficult to get an appropriate benchmark. The overall aggregate *monthly* rate reported by the US Bureau of Labor Statistics was about 3.3 percent for mid-2015.
6 The latest numbers (www.pmn.org.pk/assets/articles/MicroNOTE%2013%20-%20Microfinance%20Industry%20Salary%20Survey.pdf) we were able to find on staff salaries for micro-finance institutions (MFIs) in Pakistan suggest that Akhuwat is paying way below market rates for all field staff management levels. In 2011, the MFI average salaries for upper, middle and lower management were Rs. 110,000, Rs. 43,000 and Rs. 15,000 respectively. The corresponding salary bands for field staff at Akhuwat as per the Human Resource Manual were respectively Rs. 10,000–30,000 (area manager), Rs. 10,000–20,000 (branch manager) and Rs. 7,500–15,000 (unit manager/loan officer) for 2015.
7 Branch offices had and exercised policy discretion to suit the local context. For example, the extent of use of the group or guarantor method for loan approval varied.
8 See Harper (2011, p. 25). We personally did not hear any field staff member or head staff member make this statement.
9 See Chapter 6 for survey responses pertaining to this sub-section.
10 A Case Study by Malcolm Harper, Akhuwat, Journey of Hope, www.akhuwat.org.pk/akhuwatcaseStudy.asp (consulted July 5, 2016).
11 The pressure to expand also comes from the highest levels of political power. For example, the Governor of Khyber Pukhtoon Khwa Province (KPK) wanted Akhuwat to establish a presence in the Federally Administered Tribal Areas (FATA) since this was perceived as an initiative that would be welcomed in the conservative culture prevailing there. This tribal area for the most part lived by its own laws and parts were subject to military action to weed out militants during our fieldwork. The expansion into remote Gilgit-Baltistan, that includes the three highest mountain ranges in the world (Himalayas, Hindukush and Karakorum), no doubt resulted from such pressure. Even so, in the words of the executive director "expansion has been rapid, and many people have raised eyebrows, but it is still very cautious and systematic."
12 www.akhuwat.org.pk/reports.asp.
13 All such contracts are won via competitive bidding. According to the executive director, 7 percent is lower than the approximately 10 percent it takes to manage the fund (a competitor bid was about 14 percent), and so it is subsidizing the government as part of this public-private partnership.
14 Rs. 36 million was provided by Care International, UK, for the Credit Pool revolving fund, and so Akhuwat may have revised its policy on not accepting foreign donations.

15 The executive director noted that the lack of internet connectivity among current and ex-members was a problem with regards to staying in touch.
16 The executive director pointed the bank would be modeled after the JAK interest-free cooperative banking in Sweden.
17 We have refrained from expressing our views on issues but we support Akhuwat's policy of encouraging women into the public domain.

References

Haque, Z. 1995. *Riba: The Moral Economy of Usury, Interest and Profit* (Kuala Lumpur: Ikraq).

Harper, M. 2011. "It Sometimes Makes Sense to Break the Rules," Chapter 2 in "Akhuwat Exploring New Horizons in Microfinance," Conference Proceedings, March 24, 2011, www.akhuwat.org.pk/books/Exploring%20New%20Horizons%20in%20Microfinance.pdf, consulted July 19, 2016.

Khan, S. R. 1987. *Profit and Loss Sharing: An Economic Analysis of an Islamic Financial System* (Karachi: Oxford University Press).

Section 3
Summary and conclusions

Akhuwat is run by a leader (Dr. Amjad Saqib) that, if we are any judge of character, is good to the core. He is charismatic, interacts with and inspires field staff at all levels, evokes a devoted following, and is a religious man with a progressive vision. He also is a pragmatist who understands that he is now leading something that is bigger than he could have imagined and has the ability to craft and implement policies to realize the vision and mission of the organization. His vision has evolved in a way that ensures organizational sustainability (more on this later), and this genius is evident in the field. Operationalizing the organizational social philosophy ensures a good recovery and also sustains the organization and spreads the social philosophy.

The vision in a nutshell is to realize *bhaichara* or brotherhood, the literal meaning of Akhuwat. Conceptually it can be better understood in a historical context as 'empathy' and 'social solidarity' (Chapter 1). One unit manager's understanding of this social philosophy, which we have paraphrased, was particularly notable. He said we have been put on earth to help each other; God's might is not affected by worship or the lack of it. One could think of this organization as the Good Samaritan, i.e. humanity's keeper. Accordingly, its mission is to enable as many entrepreneurial poor to become self-sustaining as its funds permit.

The progressiveness of the vision is embodied in the founder's teachings to the field staff that when dealing with borrowers, they must "turn the other cheek." Thus the most remarkable success of the organization is the treatment of borrowers by field staff in a way that embodies the spirit of empathy. In turn, this spirit of empathy is echoed by the borrowers in explaining why they gave back (Chapter 2 and 6). How deeply the teachings regarding empathy is internalized in the staff and the borrowers can be assessed to some extent by the findings of survey research, group discussions and key informant interviews.

We visited 5 percent of the branches and randomly sampled 1.5 percent respectively of all current and ex-borrowers. This is a small sample because we were determined to do the fieldwork ourselves rather than rely on a hired survey team. The size of the organization (about 48,000 borrowers and ex-borrowers in mid-2015) and our limitations in terms of time and funds constrained the scope of this study. Overall we managed to interview 267 individuals, 78 ex-borrowers, which represented a response rate of 58.3 percent (see Chapter 6 for explanations regarding the response rate).

In our visits in almost six weeks of fieldwork to 13 branches we came across very few individuals who did not praise the organization without reservation for the good work it is doing in assisting the poorest by providing interest free credit. Eight-five percent rated staff conduct as very good, and another 9 percent rated it as 'good.' Similarly, 88 percent rated the procedures and also the organization as very good, and another 8 percent as good.

Of those that rated the organization highly, about a third did so because they did not charge interest and a fifth because the organization and its staff work in a dedicated manner to help the poor. It is no wonder that the organization had the confidence to provide us complete and open access and allowed us to conduct confidential interviews and group discussions. In the past we had not been allowed open access, without field staff present, by other development NGOs to conduct an institutional analysis and aborted two studies for this reason.

Nine-tenths responded that the loan had contributed to a substantial increase in household income, and we cite other statistics in Chapter 6 and 7 that clearly indicate to us that the organization has been very successful in enhancing the well-being of loan recipients based on several criteria.

We used statistics on conventional indicators of success such as growth of operations (branches, beneficiaries, and loan portfolio), recovery rates and donations. Imitation in the private sector is often viewed as a marker of business success. The same could be deemed to be the case in the civil society sector. Many individuals and organizations have in the short period of Akhuwat's existence (2002–2018) contacted it to replicate its approach to microcredit and the organization has encouraged such replication with technical assistance. Appendix 5.5 lists organizations that have adopted Akhuwat's lending philosophy and methods.

In Chapter 6 we evaluate Akhuwat's success based on beneficiary perceptions as another criterion in evaluating success. If those that Akhuwat purports to serve are satisfied on various counts with the service that the organization claims to deliver, then it could indeed be deemed to be a success. As indicated above, this was overwhelmingly the case. Even more important in assessing an organization is exploring whether or not it attains it vision as encapsulated in its founding documents. In Chapter 6 we assess

Summary and conclusions 159

how successful it is in attaining its stated vision, and in Chapter 7 we assess whether or not it is successful in promoting self-entrepreneurship, a core element in its mission statement. It both cases we conclude that it has been remarkably successful. Last but not least, we evaluate Akhuwat's success in terms of our working definition of altruism as defined in Chapter 2. This is critical since Akhuwat claims to have built its organization around this core concept.

Our focus in this research was therefore institutional rather than an impact assessment since this is an organization that is seeking to bring about institutional change as a mechanism to realize systemic change.[1] The institutional change is both a foundation for the systemic change and the norms and values based on empathy and social solidarity are also an ends in and of themselves.

As indicated, the institutional change it seeks is at the level of changing values by promoting empathy at the grassroots level. The objective is to do this at a wide enough scale to create a better society. No doubt the use of interest free microcredit as a mechanism to attain this objective is fortuitous for it. While it is religiously driven and sincere and meets a basic human right of access to credit for the poorest, it also provides the organization a high likelihood for success.

Its reported recovery rate is as high as it is (99.95, January 5, 2018) because of the enormous goodwill generated among borrowers.[2] These borrowers want to reciprocate by paying the loans back conscientiously to a religiously sincere organization that they consider has helped them in a self-less way with no ulterior motive. Given the high level of religiosity among the population and the hatred for interest, the organization has struck a chord among the population and the staff.[3] Many potential borrowers initially wonder "what the catch is" but then turn away in droves from other interest-based NGO credit organizations to borrow from Akhuwat.

One could argue that the enormous goodwill at the grassroots level that we witnessed and documented is nothing special. After all, it is free money, so what is there to complain about? However free money needs to be recovered if the organization is to protect its credit pool, and what makes it special is the courtesy with which the organization does this and the teaching regarding empathy and social solidarity that it imparts in the process. Across the board, borrowers echoed this social philosophy and argued for the right of the organization to put systems in place for checks and monitoring to ensure the money is well used and recovered.

One could also take a cynical view of the organizational teaching regarding empathy and social solidarity since it is aligned with its goals of attaining a high recovery rate and protecting its credit pool. We prefer to view its teachings in this regard as an example of enlightened self-interest. Of course the organization does not rely only on promoting empathy and social solidarity among borrowers for high recovery rates. Stringent borrower selection criteria, pragmatic lending practices including monitoring, an incredibly streamlined organizational structure, a sensible set of evolving policies and a dedicated staff do the rest.

Not all the young unit managers that represent the core and foundation of the organization are on a mission. For some it is a job. However, for many the missionary zeal leads them to forego higher salaries and work to sustain an organization that they feel represents a win-win in that they get paid to do good work. This zeal is evocative of the core cadre of a communist party trying to bring out systemic change. However, the revolution they have in mind is not to attain a classless society in terms of material differences. While Islam rejects social class as depicted by mosque culture, it does accept that material differences can arise both from effort or inheritance. These material differences are then seen as a mutual test for individuals. The more prosperous are deemed to be tested by the less prosperous and vice versa by mutual service (43:32). The more prosperous are also expected to behave in a socially enlightened way by giving to society based on Qur'anic prescriptions.

Dr. Amjad Saqib's view is that while in many parts of the country there may be a dearth of financial capital, there is no scarcity of a community driven culture of hospitality and solidarity or social capital. He views capitalism to have an element of "dog-eat-dog" ethic which can erode this social capital. The social philosophy Akhuwat represents is viewed in this regard as an antidote to this destructive capitalist ethic.

While the leadership has a progressive vision, it does partner with others with a more conservative religious interpretation but who share the organization's goal of eliminating interest-based microcredit. So far, we see no signs for concern in that realizing Akhuwat or empathy is the dominant ethic embodying the organization. However, retaining this dominant vision could be a challenge when partnering with others with a different vision.

One quibble we noted in Chapter 8 is that the organization receives "interest" on its investments. We have adopted the interpretation whereby *riba*, which bans interest and other forms of social extraction, extends to banks charging interest on loans beyond the inflation rate plus administrative fee. Also as explained in Chapter 8, the increase that they charge is not based on incurring either human effort or risk, i.e. giving counter-value. Further, there is an asymmetric power equation between the two parties to the contract. However, the organization views the taking or giving any form of interest as banned and so drawing a fixed return on its investments is suggestive of inconsistency in our view even if it is endorsed by a bank's *sharia* (Islamic law) Committee.[4]

It has been noted by Harper (Chapter 8), that Akhuwat has turned the traditional microcredit model on its head and that its concern is with the self-sufficiency of the poor borrowers rather than the sustainability of the organization. While Akhuwat can pursue this course in the short-term, it will disappear as fast as it appeared without a solid plan for its own sustainability. Currently, the founder's remarkable fund-raising ability has built a large credit pool. However, the main credit pool is based on tapping political administrations at the Federal and Provincial level[5] that identify with its vision and mission and are also reaping political dividends for the good work Akhuwat is doing. As a percentage of its liability base, voluntary contributions were 15 percent in 2016. This needs to be at a much higher level if Akhuwat is to sustain its current rate of expansion (see Chapter 4).

In our view, if it can convert itself into a member-based organization and tap the enormous goodwill among its ex-borrowers[6] and the broader public its growth will be more organic rather than discrete and dependent on micro-finance management contracts it can win from friendly political administrations. Such organic growth, as is the case for the Edhi Foundation, will probably make it a very major presence in poverty alleviation in Pakistan. Akhuwat will probably also make a notable change in promoting empathy and social solidarity in Pakistan and put forward a microcredit model for at least other Islamic countries to emulate.

Our emphasis on 'empathy' and 'social solidarity' rather than *bhaichara* or 'brotherhood' is deliberate. Muslim countries will continue to hold themselves back in the race among nations if they treat women as second class citizens. They need to systemically tap the talent of this half of the population: a project that other developed and developing nations have embarked on with varying success.[7] Here again Akhuwat has shown the way by lending to women in a way that they have control over the use of the funds and also welcoming them into public spaces.

Notes

1 See Appendix 7.1 for our reasoning on why an impact assessment of Akhuwat would be deeply flawed.
2 "Overview/Impact/Progress Report," www.akhuwat.org.pk/progress_report.asp (consulted January 31, 2018).
3 Borrowers share the organizational vision of eradicating interest-based microfinance because it is viewed as a scourge based on religious edicts. They also associate it with the mosque, given the check distribution ceremony is in the mosque, and are comfortable with that. Some even refer to it as the *maulvi* (religious leader) bank.
4 One prominent member of a Steering Committee equated our view of *riba* as the equivalent of self-medication. He thought that just as the population relies on doctors for medication, they need to rely on Islamic scholars for religious

interpretation. The problem of course is that interpretations of religious scholars can also vary.
5 The reference here is to the Punjab which is the most populous and prosperous Pakistani province.
6 Currently ex-borrowers are considered closed cases. Given the enormous goodwill we found for the organization even among ex-borrowers, we think that a more systematic effort to keep lines of communications open with them and at least to tap those that have prospered would assist with fund raising.
7 Pakistan is showing signs of progress in this regard. The World Bank data for Pakistan shows a rise in female labor force participation from 12.5 percent in 1995 to 24.6 percent in 2016 (Pakistan Female labor force participation – data, chart www.theglobaleconomy.com/Pakistan/Female_labor_force_participation/). We estimated (from informal head office staff responses) female staff as a percentage of the total for Akhuwat to be 3.5 percent in 2016. Thus, Akhuwat has a way to go in catching up with the rest of the country in this regard. This is particularly the case at the field level. One recommendation from the female Focus Group Discussion at Bhulwal was having separate branches for men and women because the male staff presence (or lack of female staff) made it uncomfortable for them to go to the branch.

Index

afterlife consumption 15
Akhuwat: altruism as framework of x, 6, 27–34 (*see also* altruism); *bhaichara* and 17; *bhaichara vs.* social solidarity 143, 161; diversification of 6–7, 35n2, 117–118; evaluation of 10; expansion of xi–xii; founding of 1; as "giving economy" 11; government support of 8–9; *Mwakhaat-i-Medina* and 17; operational issues xi–xii, 10; organizational culture 31–32; origin of name x; *Qarz-e-Hassn* and xi; view of microcredit 27; vision and mission of 1; vision of 75; *see also* Akhuwat microcredit model
Akhuwat Book Bank Program 30–31
Akhuwat Clothes Bank 7, 27, 30–31
Akhuwat Dreams Project 33–34
Akhuwat Educational Assistance Program 27, 32–33
Akhuwat Food Bank Program 30–31
Akhuwat Health Services (AHS) 27, 28–29, 33
Akhuwat Institute of Social Enterprise & Management 6
Akhuwat Internship and Leadership Program 7, 27
Akhuwat *Khwaja Sira* Socio-Economic Rehabilitation Program 27–30, 35n3
Akhuwat microcredit model 57–69, 75–116; as alternative to conventional models 61–64; *bhaichara vs.* hierarchy in 138; concerns about 142–143, 149; expansion of 66, 146, 155n11; feminist critique of 94; field research method 75–77; funds donated since inception 68; goodwill toward 145, 146, 148, 159; guiding principles of 58; households served by 57; impact assessment issues 132–133; and imposition of moral values with public money 145; inclusivity of 58; inclusivity *vs.* selectivity of 138, 154n3; and Islamic ban on *riba* (*see riba*); lending methodology 79–80; loan amounts 60–61; loan case histories and 120–130, 133n6; macroeconomic impacts of 120, 130; mission achievement 118–119; mission and vision 57–58; as model of labor leverage 119–120; and monitoring of loans 139; operational issues of 59–60, 138–141; organization of 59–61; outreach by 59–60; percentage distribution of loan products 69; policy changes 141–142; and promotion of interfaith harmony 58; recovery rates since inception 67; replications of 64, 70, 120; research design and sampling 77–79, 115n4; reservations about and ideological inconsistencies 142–145; ROSCAs *vs.* 114; staff behavior and policies 139–141; staff salaries and turnover rates 140, 155n5, 155n6; study findings 81–87 (*see also* study findings); success of 58–59, 80–81, 89–93, 158–159;

164 Index

summary of findings 130–131; sustainability of 145–146, 161; transgender community and 143
Akhuwat Transgender Rehabilitation Program 27–30
Akhuwat University, plans for 27, 32–33
Akram, Shahzad xii
Ali, Mehreen xii
altruism 14–24; as central Akhuwat principle x, 6; impure 15, 16; individual *versus* organizational 25; utility function and 16; working definition of 20–21, 22
altruism in Pakistan 25–36; study of 25–26
Amir-ul-Momineen 5
Amjad Saqib *see* Saqib, Amjad
Ansari, Natasha ix–x, xii
Awan, Kazim Raza xii
Ayub Khan, Mohammed 4

Bangladesh: microcredit studies in 40, 42–43, 45, 47–48; *see also* Grameen Bank; Yunus, Muhammad
banking, interest-free 4
behenchara (sisterhood) xiiin7
bhaichara (brotherhood) 17, 87, 92, 137, 138, 143, 148, 157, 161
Book Bank Program 30–31
Borrowers: case histories of 120–130, 133n6; enabling self-sufficiency of 17; interviews of 76, 78, 80–82; moral guidance for 64; and perceptions of Akhuwat 89–93; staff treatment of 157–158; suggestions from 146–148; support for 63–64; *see also* focus groups
borrowers to donors principle 17, 19–22, 58, 61–62, 75

case histories 120–130, 133n6
Cheema, Aneeq 31
children, Dreams Project and 33–34
Collective for Social Science Research xii
commercialization of 44; criticisms of 1; critiques of 7, 8, 37–56, 41–48; debt treadmill and 49–50; evaluating success of 46–47; feminist critique of 8

community building 7; *see also* social solidarity
Consultative Group to Assist the Poor (CGAP) 45
conventional microcredit: as agent for neo-liberalism 87; Akhuwat's alternative to 1
credit pool: contributions to 146, 155n14; funding sources of 149; sustaining 92
critical thinking skills, Rabtt and 27, 31–32

debt treadmill, conventional microcredit and 49–50
Dewar-e-Akhuwat 30
Diabetes Center 33
Donations: amount of 58–59, 68; anonymous *vs.* public 94, 147, 149, 150–151; borrower attitudes toward 83–84, 88, 150–151; encouragement of 58; policy for 60

economics, Islamic 117
economy, Islamization of 4–5
education: Akhuwat commitment to 6–7, 32–33; Rabtt and 31; threats to 35n9
empathy, creating 17, 20, 22, 27, 75, 82–85, 92, 94, 120, 132, 140, 142–143, 157, 159
entrepreneurship, in conventional microcredit *versus* Akhuwat 9, 46–47, 65
ethical principles, Islamic 61–62; *see also* Islamic giving; Qur'an

faith-inspired giving 14–16, 22n1
fatwas, Qur'an and 5, 12n10
Fazlur, Rahman 4
female empowerment: conventional microcredit and 47; and neo-liberal appropriation of microcredit 41–43; *see also* women
feminism, conventional microcredit and 8
field research 75–77; design and sampling 77–79, 115n4, 115n7; response biases and 76–77
financialization, conventional microcredit and 43–46

Index 165

financialization and 43–46; gender inequality and 42–43; governing assumptions of 9; interest rates of x; neo-liberal appropriation of 37–39, 41–43; as poverty alleviation *versus* financial sustainability 45; supportive studies of 39–41
focus groups: discussion questions for 108; findings from 87–89; gender differences in 88–89; size and gender of participants 109
Food Bank Program 30–31
Fountain House 7, 28, 29, 30
fundamentalism, *versus* modernist/ progressive views 3–4

gender inequality, conventional microcredit and 42–43
"Girls at *Dhabas*" initiative xiin7
giving *see* donations; faith-inspired giving; Islamic giving
giving economy 11
giving society, characteristics of 34
Grameen Bank 9, 38, 44
group lending: attitudes toward 131, 142, 147; *versus* individual loans 84–85
Gynae Clinic 33

Hadood Ordinance 4
health care, Akhuwat's commitment to 33
hijab, public opinion and 3
household harmony, fostering 85–86
household income, loan impact on 118
human nature, Qur'anic view of 17–18
human potential, Akhuwat's commitment to 32

ijtihad, orthodox view of 4
infaq (voluntary giving) *see* voluntary giving (*infaq*)
Islam: Akhuwat's understanding of 6; values *versus* practice in ix; *see also* Qur'an
Islamic economic philosophy 117
Islamic giving 17–20; anonymity and 18–19, 21; forms of 17, 23n6;

practical issues in 19–20; Qur'anic guidance for 18
Islamic microfinance, country case studies on 48–50

Jafarey, Saqib 11
Jameel, Mehlab 35n3

Khan, Shahrukh, background of ix
Khuda Ka Liye 11–12n1
khwaja sira community *see* transgender (*khwaja sira*) community
Kiran Foundation 32

labor-capital relations, innovative model of 119–120
lending cycle, goal of 117–118
literacy rate 35n8
loan eligibility, criteria used for 79–80
loan recovery: strategy for 118–119; *see also* recovery rates; repayment
loan treadmill, avoiding 86–87, 94

Mansoor, Shoaib 12n1
Microcredit: conventional organizations of (*see* conventional microcredit); *versus* microfinance 51n1
microcredit movement, poverty alleviation and 38
mosques, role in Akhawat microlending 17, 31, 59, 61, 63, 88–89, 136, 139, 147
motivation: faith-inspired giving and 18–19; for giving 19–21, 23n13, 26; views of 15–16
mudarabah, profit-sharing and 49
musharika, profit-sharing and 49
Mwakhaat-i-Medina, Akhawat principles from 17

neo-liberalism: and appropriation of microcredit 37–39, 41–43; impacts on female empowerment 41–43; negative social outcomes of 50–51
NGOs, Bangladeshi 47–48, 52n14

orthodox religion, *versus* modernist/ progressive views 3–4

Pakistan: altruism in (*see* altruism in Pakistan); government of ix; Islamization of 4; philanthropy in 25–27
Pakistan Center for Philanthropy 26
Pakistani society, and separation of religion and politics 3
Pakistan Poverty Alleviation Fund (PPAF) 8–9
philanthropy in Pakistan, legislation and studies pertaining to 25–26
policy issues 135–156
poverty alleviation: conventional microcredit and 8; organizational agendas undermining 47–48; as original intent of microcredit movement 38; subordination to financial sustainability 45
profit maximizing, Qur'anic teachings and 23n10
progressive views, *versus* fundamentalism religious views 3–4
Prophet, Qur'anic verses on role of 5, 12n9
Punjab Government's Public Schools Support Program 32

Qarz-e-Hassn (benevolent loans) 49
Qarz-e-Hassn xi, 58
Qur'an: on Prophet's role 5, 12n9; references to giving 17 (*see also* Islamic giving); on use of force 5; view of earthly life 18; view of human nature 17–18

Rabtt 27, 31–32, 35n10, 36n12
randomized control trials (RCTs): problems with 10–11; on voluntary giving 150–153
Rasheed, Fatima 22n1
recovery rates 59, 67, 159
religion, and separation from politics 3
religious decrees, effects on personal life 3
religious spaces, role in Akhawat microlending 17, 31, 59, 61, 63, 88–89, 136, 139, 147
repayment: motivation for 63–64; record of 118–119; social solidarity as factor in 17

repayment policy 60; in conventional microcredit 48; forgiveness and 61
research *see* field research
response biases 76–77
riba: Akhuwat and xi; borrower attitudes toward 159, 161n3; broadened definition of 143–144, 149, 160, 161n4; elimination of 75; Islamic ban on xi
ROSCA (Rotating Saving and Credit Association), *versus* Akhuwat microcredit model 93, 114

Sadeque, Najma 8
Saqib, Amjad x, 17, 25; interview with 90–91; message of 142–143; view of Pakistani social capital 160; vision and character of 157
Sarwar, Imran 31, 36n12
schools, Islamization of 4
self-help groups, NGO-initiated 40, 51n6
self-sufficiency 117–134, 158; as Akhuwat goal 118–119; labor-capital relations model and 119–120; loan case-histories and 120–130
Sen, A. K. 15–16, 21
Sharif, Nawaz 5
sisterhood (*behenchara*) xiiin7
Smith, V. 16, 21
social capital, conventional microcredit and 7
social harmony, creating 83–84, 115n11
social legislation: under orthodox regimes 4–5; religion's impact on 3
social solidarity 161; aspirations for 17, 20, 22, 27, 75, 82–85, 92, 94, 120, 132, 140, 142–143, 157, 159
staff: behavior of 86, 115n13; borrower perceptions of 90, 94; idealism of 92, 160; moral guidance for 64; non-local 140–141; salaries and turnover rates 59, 140, 155n5
study findings 81–87; background 81–82; business appraisal forms 113; key informant interviews and 110–111; sample distribution by branch 95; social appraisal forms 112; structured questionnaire for

96–107; on success of organization 82–87; summary of 93–94

Taliban 5, 35n9
Theory of Moral Sentiments (Smith) 15
transgender (*khwaja sira*) community: Akhuwat programs for 27–30, 34; reintegration of 7; social exclusion and prejudice against 29; violence against 35n5
Transgender Rehabilitation Program 27

utilitarianism, broad definition of 14–15
utility function, altruism and 16
utility maximization model, extension of 15, 23n4

voluntarism: Akhuwat and 6; in Pakistan *versus* U. S. 26–27; spirit of 58

voluntary giving (*infaq*) 17, 25, 61; borrower attitudes toward 144–145; proposed RCT on 150–153; *see also* donations; Islamic giving

Weisskopf, Tom ix
Women: and access to public spaces 148; Bangladeshi NGOs and 47–48; in Muslim countries 161, 162n7; and neo-liberal appropriation of microcredit 41–43; reproductive health services for 33
World Bank, and hijacking of microcredit movement 38–39, 45, 50

Yunus, Muhammad 38, 90, 116n18; and "entrepreneurship for all" claim 46–47; Nobel Peace Prize and 44
Yusufzai, Malala 35n9

zakat tax 4
Zia-ul-Haq ix, 4, 5